Our world is desperate for healing. Would y  would look like if the church embraced its] nations – even in the midst of suffering and

We need more churches like Resurrec̶ ̶ ̶ ̶ ̶ ̶ ̶ ̶ ̶ ̶ ̶ (RCB) and leaders like Pastor Hikmat to lead the way in discipling the nations with the hope of Christ. In Lebanon, RCB is on the front lines sharing God's truth with love to the refugees from Syria and Iraq. In every circumstance, the church remains committed to make Christ known as our only hope and salvation – even as the world around is being torn apart.

Following Jesus in Turbulent Times is a practical handbook for developing leaders, church planters and growing members. It shares stories of lives transformed by Christ within the church as well as the community. We're blessed to serve alongside Pastor Hikmat and RBC as they put into action *The Purpose Driven Church* and *The PEACE Plan.*

Pastor Rick Warren
Founding Pastor, Saddleback Church, Lake Forest, California, USA
Author of *The Purpose Driven Life* and *The Purpose Driven Church*

There is no more powerful witness to the truth of the gospel than sacrificial love for "the least of these" in our world. And this is the witness that's most effective in the war-torn Middle East during the worst humanitarian crisis of our time. I've visited Pastor Hikmat Kashouh and observed Resurrection Church Beirut's courageous outreach to Syrian refugees. It is an inspiring example of how the demonstration of Jesus's unconditional love can change hearts – and ultimately change the world. Reading this book will fill you with hope and equip you and your church to share God's great love for all people, wherever you live.

Richard Stearns
President Emeritus, World Vision USA
Author of *The Hole in Our Gospel*

One of the joys of my life has been the pleasure of meeting Dr Hikmat Kashouh. The church I pastor is involved in a covenant partnership with Hikmat and his church. He is a man of enormous integrity and grace. His skilled leadership is an example for all who want to lead well. His work among the hurting refugees and people through Resurrection Church in Beirut, Lebanon, is an inspiration to us all. Christian leaders and pastors from around the world can learn much from what he has learned and now practices. After almost forty years in ministry, I still believe that the local church is the hope of the world. Read this book and you can discover what may happen in your context as well.

David Chadwick
Senior Pastor, Forest Hill Church, Charlotte, North Carolina, USA

It is my privilege and honor to endorse Pastor Hikmat's book, *Following Jesus in Turbulent Times*. The book is written having the Syrian refugee crisis and their presence in Lebanon as its background. Following Jesus in turbulent times requires a searching of our own hearts, and a rediscovery of the power of the gospel and the wonderful potential of our communities to serve God and others. Pastor Hikmat's book and his own personal testimony so beautifully presented in the book will help all of us to run our individual races victoriously.

I have no doubts that those who are going to read this wonderful book will be inspired, challenged and blessed.

Elias Dantas
Founder and International Facilitator, Global Kingdom Partnerships Network
Executive Director, Nyack College, New York, USA

From the humble and traumatic experiences in his early life, Rev Dr Hikmat Kashouh provides invaluable insights and wisdom from his personal journey of salvation and forgiveness through to his present leadership of a thriving ministry that lovingly and sacrificially reaches out to touch the lives of Arabs. The advice he shares comes not just from personal experiences but his passion to boldly proclaim Jesus, live by his example and invite people to follow him. I have personally witnessed the amazing work Dr Kashouh leads at Resurrection Church Beirut and met some of his dedicated co-workers and beautiful converts who are testament to this great work. I highly recommend this book to anyone working among Arabs.

Lord and Lady Robert & Tracie Edmiston
Founder & Chairman, and Executive Trustee, CV Global

The church in Lebanon is on the cutting edge of one of the most remarkable moves of the Holy Spirit in the region. As a result, they are having to rethink what it means to be a church, how to do missions within their context and culture, and how to make disciples who are culturally and locally relevant. It is

Following Jesus in Turbulent Times

Disciple-Making in the Arab World

Hikmat Kashouh

Langham
GLOBAL LIBRARY

© 2018 Hikmat Kashouh

Published 2018 by Langham Monographs
An imprint of Langham Publishing
www.langhampublishing.org

Langham Publishing and its imprints are a ministry of Langham Partnership

Langham Partnership
PO Box 296, Carlisle, Cumbria, CA3 9WZ, UK
www.langham.org

ISBNs:
Print: 978-1-78368-513-4
ePub: 978-1-78368-514-1
Mobi: 978-1-78368-515-8
PDF: 978-1-78368-516-5

Hikmat Kashouh has asserted his right under the Copyright, Designs and Patents Act, 1988 to be identified as the Author of this work.

British Library Cataloguing-in-Publication Data
A catalogue record for this book is available from the British Library

ISBN: 9781783685134

Cover & Book Design: projectluz.com

Langham Partnership actively supports theological dialogue and an author's right to publish but does not necessarily endorse the views and opinions set forth here or in works referenced within this publication, nor can we guarantee technical and grammatical correctness. Langham Partnership does not accept any responsibility or liability to persons or property as a consequence of the reading, use or interpretation of its published content.

To my parents, Najah and Noha Kashouh
To the true heroes whose stories of transformation are mentioned in this book
To all RCB's pastors, staff, and life-group leaders
With Love and Gratitude

not an easy task to balance Arab culture and sensitivities with an intrusive global culture easily accessible through digital media. It is within such a context that Dr Kashouh writes from the depth of his experience of shepherding and growing a local congregation while searching the Scriptures for principles and models. He blends his western experience with a strong appreciation of local realities. There are very few books written about doing ministry through a local church and making disciples in the Middle East and the Arab world. This is an invaluable book for anyone wanting to understand or minister in this part of the world.

Rupen Das
National Director, Canadian Bible Society
Research Professor,
Tyndale University College and Seminary, Toronto, Ontario, Canada

This book, written by Dr Hikmat Kashouh, is one of the best books on discipleship for Muslim background believers. This is a very precious book for making disciples in the Arab world and beyond, as well as helping new Christians to grow in their spiritual life. I totally recommend this book as a necessary resource for every disciple who lives in the Islamic context and for churches around the globe who work and serve cross-culturally.

Eddy Leo
Apostolic Team Ministry Leader, Abbalove Ministries, Indonesia

To minister to people who are in need regardless of their cultural background is a call every Christ-follower ought to take. In *Following Jesus in Turbulent Times*, Pastor Hikmat provides exemplary insights on what it means to build a church community that impacts and serves others for Christ. He speaks not just from theory but from actual experiences.

This book is filled with stories of faith, transformation, and selfless service that will surely inspire you to move out of our comfort zones and care for those who are troubled and in pain. Pastor Hikmat highlights that as Christians move out of our comfortable way of life, our devotion for others is transformational and will outweigh any sacrifice.

May this book stir in your heart a deep desire to love and disciple others as we carry out our mission to go and make disciples of all nations.

Peter Tan-Chi
Founder and Senior Pastor,
Christ's Commission Fellowship, Manila, Philippines

This book is an amazing record of abiding faith and God's amazing faithfulness in turbulent times. It doubles up as a remarkable manual on evangelism, discipleship and church growth that is tested on the anvil of sufferings. It offers hope to all in spite of the challenges, and reinforces the belief that the church is indeed the hope of the nations! Something for everyone to be soundly instructed and inspired by Pastor Hikmat!

Daniel Ho
Founding Senior Pastor
Damansara Utama Methodist Church, Malaysia

Following Jesus in Turbulent Times

GLOBAL LIBRARY

CONTENTS

Foreword

What exactly are we trying to accomplish?

In the words popularized by best-selling author Stephen Covey (but widely attributed in the 1940s to Edith Wharton), we are caught "in the thick of thin things." Failing to distinguish the essential from the non-essential, we have the propensity to major on the minor. And having become accustomed to the whirlwind of busy activities, we often fail to ask the important question: "What exactly are we trying to accomplish?"

There is a critical discipleship deficit in the church today.

- Extended spiritual infancy abounds.
- Holiness is a forsaken word.
- Carnality robs the church of her integrity and authority.
- Worldliness and immorality.
- Spiritual consumerism and compromise.
- Biblical illiteracy and shallowness.
- Broken marriages and church fights.

All these are critical warning signs that something is desperately amiss! We must get back to basics. To advance the global cause of Christ, we must abide in Him!

Therefore, I have no doubt that **authentic discipleship** (i.e. following Jesus, and becoming Christ-centred and Christ-like) is the cardinal mandate for the church; and that **intentional disciplemaking** (i.e. reproducing Christ-like followers of Jesus) is the core mission of the church.

There are many good things that a local church might do. But her cardinal mandate should not be compromised, nor her core mission neglected. The key is intentionality.

Establishing such an intentional disciplemaking church is vital. And our job is not to try to manufacture (or worse, manipulate) "success" by our programs and formulas. Rather, it is to seek the agenda of God, in the light of His Word, and to stay faithful to it.

That's exactly what Hikmat Kashouh, the senior pastor of Resurrection Church Beirut (RCB), has done. He has sought the agenda of God and stayed faithful to it, even in the turbulent world he ministers in. Regardless of the circumstances, he has demonstrated a steadfast passion for reaching the lost and making disciples!

Pastor Hikmat ministers in a most challenging world. I read these heart-breaking words in his book and it moved me deeply:

> *A woman told how she was forced to stand and watch as members of her family were sexually abused and killed in front of her eyes. She was told that if she showed any emotion or uttered a word, she too would be killed. Children have seen their parents die, and little girls have watched as men raped their mothers. One woman was fleeing with her daughter when a sniper shot the child. Another woman was carrying her three-year-old son when he was killed in her arms by a bullet.* (p. 12)

Yet, God is on the move! In this captivating book, *Following Jesus in Turbulent Times: Disciple-Making in the Arab Word,* Pastor Hikmat recounts the incredible grace of God despite the pain and brokenness. People are coming to Jesus! And lives are transformed!

Shortly before the war began in Syria, God highlighted to Pastor Hikmat and his church leaders the need to serve the marginalized. Under his outstanding leadership, their arms were opened to the refugees with the love of Jesus. Refugees are not despised, or seen only as objects of charity or merely as potential converts. Rather, they are treated with dignity and respect; as people created in the image of God to be loved in the name of Jesus!

Intentional acts of kindness were offered, with no strings attached, until the refugees themselves asked, "Why are you doing this for us?" And many were thus brought to Christ and discipled!

Pastor Hikmat is an exceptional leader. What is interesting about his church is this: of the 1,300 regular attendees, across three campuses, about seventy percent of these are refugees! For a pastor with a Baptist background and a PhD in theology from Birmingham University, I am delighted that the word "status quo" is obviously not in his leadership dictionary! He boldly leads this exciting disciplemaking church.

"I no longer see leadership in terms of power but in terms of love and caring for others," he insightfully wrote. Being a true storyteller, Pastor Hikmat gives us a compelling narrative of changed lives and transformation. Reading this faithful account would deepen our faith, strengthen our hope and establish our love to reach and disciple the lost!

Following Jesus in Turbulent Times is indeed inspiring in its stories of transformation. It is balanced in its perspective, wise in its principles and efficacious in its recommendations. Behind the amazing stories are instructive models and strategies, presented with a keen pastoral wisdom. And these are not just theories but principles and best practices gleaned from the trenches.

I have been very blessed in reading this inspiring and instructive book. It is a stirring book and a page-turner. I most gladly recommend it to you!

Edmund Chan
Leadership Mentor, Covenant Evangelical Free Church
Founder, Global Alliance of Intentional Disciplemaking Churches

Acknowledgements

It is impossible to write a book like this without formally acknowledging the outstanding work of the pastors and leaders of Resurrection Church Beirut, whose faithful life and ministry stands behind every sentence and paragraph. I am indebted to all of them. I am also indebted to my predecessor, Pastor Ghassan Khalaf, who trusted me with Christ's bride. Thank you, too, to my wonderful church, which has entrusted me with the greatest privilege of leading and equipping its leaders, as well as teaching the Word of Truth.

I would also like to deeply thank my Muslim friends, especially those who have chosen to follow Jesus and have been a great inspiration for me.

This manuscript has gone through several revisions. I am thankful to my friends, Anika Wilson and Mike Kuhn, who took the time to read through it and make some invaluable corrections. Thank you to Langham Publishing, especially Pieter Kwant, Isobel Stevenson, and Tanya Ferdinandusz, who literally transformed the manuscript, turning it into a finished product. *Thank you!*

I am indebted to my amazing family – my wife Krista and my children, Markus, Betine, and Daniella – whose love and encouragement have sustained me throughout the journey. Finally, I am grateful to my beloved parents, who sacrificially loved my brothers, sister and me, and gave us refuge under their wings throughout sixteen years of the Lebanese civil war.

My prayer is that this book will draw a smile to my Savior's face. After all, it is the work of his hand. To him be the glory for ever and ever. Amen.

So if there is any encouragement in Christ, any comfort from love, any participation in the Spirit, any affection and sympathy, complete my joy by being of the same mind, having the same love, being in full accord and of one mind. Do nothing from selfish ambition or conceit, but in humility count others more significant than yourselves. Let each of you look not only to his own interests, but also to the interests of others. Have this mind among yourselves, which is yours in Christ Jesus, who, though he was in the form of God, did not count equality with God a thing to be grasped, but emptied himself, by taking the form of a servant, being born in the likeness of men. And being found in human form, he humbled himself by becoming obedient to the point of death, even death on a cross. Therefore God has highly exalted him and bestowed on him the name that is above every name, so that at the name of Jesus every knee should bow, in heaven and on earth and under the earth, and every tongue confess that Jesus Christ is Lord, to the glory of God the Father.

Philippians 2:1–11

1

Introduction

God is moving in the Arab world. He is speaking to people in dreams and visions, as we hear by word of mouth and through social media. I share some of these stories in this book, and would encourage people who have had similar experiences to tell their own stories, even though the listeners may be uncomfortable. When God is at work, we need to be alert so that we do not miss what he is doing.

But as more and more Arabs show an interest in following Jesus, how do we as Christians respond? How do we encourage them and disciple them? How do we help them to integrate in our churches? How do we set about building multi-ethnic, multicultural congregations that can worship together in a way that brings glory to God and shows love for all our neighbors?

These are questions that many pastors and Christian leaders are asking – not only in the West, but also in regions of the Middle East where refugees are flooding in from places like Syria and Iraq. It is not enough to point to books dealing with caring for refugees. Those books are valuable, but they do not answer the questions I want to tackle in this book, which is specifically focused on integrating believers from a Muslim background into our churches. More than that, I want to talk about how we can promote true Christian discipleship in all who attend our churches and overcome the tensions that inevitably arise when different groups meet. For it is a fundamental truth that the path of discipleship is messy. It involves ups and downs, triumphs and mistakes, times of rejoicing and times of weeping. At Resurrection Church Beirut, we seek to shepherd our people along this path by sharing and "doing life" together. I hope my own church's experiences of journeying with and discipling people from diverse backgrounds will inform and encourage pastors and leaders who are seeking to do the same.

To help you understand where I am coming from, I will begin by telling you something of my own journey of discipleship. My life has not been easy, for

I grew up during the Lebanese civil war (1975–1991), and experienced much uncertainty and pain. Yet nothing is wasted in God's kingdom, and he is now using my own experiences of war to help me serve those who are similarly in pain. I now minister in Lebanon, where 25 percent of the population are refugees from the wars in Iraq and Syria. But in our church, some 70 percent of the members are refugees. In nine years, we have gone from having ninety members to having a congregation of 1,300. We have had to learn a lot!

My hope is that the testimonies in this book and the practical examples drawn from our own experience will help you as you too set about making disciples. For that is what the church does – we are in the disciple-making business!

2

My Journey

Our relatives and neighbors were sure my mother was not going to make it, but they could not get her to the hospital due to the shelling. A sympathetic but amateurish midwife was trying frantically to help her push out a baby who didn't seem to want to see the light. Yet, by God's grace, the baby boy was born at last, and my mother proved that life and hope are greater than death and despair. My father rejoiced in the birth of his third son in twenty-three months and my aunt offered baklava to everyone.

That was in November 1975. My mother thinks I was born on the 14th and my father thinks it was on the 15th. Who knows who is right, though mothers usually know best. Even so, we celebrate my birthday on the 15th – because Dad said so!

That same year, Lebanon entered into what would become sixteen years of civil war. During the years of Syrian occupation, our people were killed, our women raped, our national resources plundered, and our dignity stolen. I remember how frightened we children were of the Syrian army at checkpoints. Our hearts would be in our mouths. Our stomachs were always upset from anxiety. Our house was bombed a number of times, relatives lost their lives, and beloved friends went missing. Ultimately, my father died as a result of the war.

My parents moved us to the mountains of Lebanon. It was not safe, but it was safer than the city. We spent most of my childhood there. My brothers and I spent our time exploring the hills and valleys, going where it seemed no one had gone before, climbing trees, picking fruit, catching colourful beetles, building tree houses and sometimes straw houses, playing football, attacking each other with fireworks, tormenting cats and flying paper kites. We never sat still. We never played computer games. We had no TV. Nature was our world and the forest our playground.

As teenagers, we also had chores to complete before going to school: doing the dishes, throwing out the rubbish, watering the vegetable garden, and feeding the few sheep we owned. This sometimes made us late for school, and explanations were embarrassing. But although we hated working in the fields, refusing to do so was not an option – because Dad said so! (I believe the current generation does not understand what "Dad said so" means.)

My two brothers and I developed a deep relationship. Like most siblings, we fought a lot, but we also learned to reconcile quickly. We discovered life together. Unlike today, asking questions about sexuality was taboo, and so we found things out on our own – sometimes using wrong methods. We developed both good and bad habits.

At home, life could be quite tense. We lived in constant fear and anxiety: fear of war, fear of conflicts at home. My father was full of anger and hate and was rarely happy and content. The relationship between my parents wasn't always harmonious or based on mutual support. Discipline was strict, and we were often smacked. My eldest brother received the brunt of Dad's strong hand. I, being the youngest, was luckier; by the time my turn came, Dad was already tired. My mother disciplined us by having us sit or kneel in a corner – once she even made us kneel on marbles.

But we did not doubt that our father loved us very much, and we loved him in return. He had some wonderful virtues: he was fearless, confident, generous, and a great storyteller. He wasn't educated, but he used to say, "I can read psychology." What he meant was that he found it easy to guess what was on someone's mind.

My mother was very servant-hearted, always making sure that all my father's needs were met. She was a wonderful cook. When we were teenagers, she loved preparing sandwiches for us – even if she got tired of the sheer number of sandwiches she had to make! She could always sense when her kids were hungry. The sight of my seven- or eight-year-old sister heading towards us was always welcome because we knew she would be carrying a bag of thyme and olive oil sandwiches. She felt very important to be providing food for her big brothers! (Today, her home is always open and she still loves to serve others.)

I did not do well at school, partly because the school moved its location a number of times. I missed a lot of classes, failed sixth grade, and dropped out of school at the age of fifteen. By that time, my father was ill and I wanted to go to work and make money to support the family. My brothers persevered with their education and after high school they continued their studies in Germany.

War, displacement, a lack of parental supervision, conflicts at home, a shortage of resources, and a lack of encouragement all contributed to my academic failure. It wasn't really my fault, and I no longer feel guilty about not finishing school. But at the time, it was a real blow to my confidence and self-esteem. I felt inadequate and stupid. So I treasured my father's words: "Son, it is ok to fail a class, but what is important is not to become a failure."

My oldest brother ended up studying mechanical engineering, but he did his practical placement long before he even started his studies. As a small boy, he loved to dismantle old washing machines, giant black-and-white TVs, and electronic items and collect the screws in small boxes. By the time he was a teenager, he was able to fix our father's car. My middle brother, now a pastor in Germany, always beat me at football, push-ups, and running – but I learned to ride a bike before he did. Despite many fights, we remained close. My brothers have helped me to become who I am today, and I am indebted to both of them.

In the summer we ran a small open market just outside our house, selling car accessories (car seat covers, radios, feather dusters, car perfumes, and car mats). We also sold petrol and bread, both of which were scarce during the war. My father used to drive his old car down the mountain to Beirut and fill up the tank. Upon his return, we would siphon off the petrol into twenty-litre containers, and sell them on the street. To obtain a few loaves of bread, we had to go to a nearby bakery before dawn and stand in the queue until midday.

One day, someone wanted to buy a car radio – the most expensive item in our shop. He asked to take it to his car to check if it worked. I agreed. Meanwhile, his friend asked me lots of questions. The first man returned, put the box on the table and promised to come back another day to buy it. In the evening, I picked up the box and realized it felt too light. Then I understood. The men had stolen the radio. How could two grown-ups have the heart to rob a child? My brothers and I felt terrible about losing so much money. However, our father was surprisingly gracious and simply advised us to learn from our mistake.

By the time I was sixteen, my uncle had helped me set up a small business in Beirut selling car parts. The business grew thanks to the good reputation enjoyed by my father and uncle. Today, in many cultures, trust needs to be earned, and can't simply be handed on from one generation to another. In the Arab world, things were different. When I was growing up and wanted to purchase parts for my shop, people would ask me, "Who is your father?" If they knew and trusted him, they would trust me too; rejecting me was rejecting my father. It was the same in Jesus's time: people wanted to know who his father was, and those who rejected him were, in fact, rejecting his Father. Today, however, it is not your father but your personal achievements, your past, your story, that count.

A New Life

My father's friend Brother Anthoon was different from anyone I knew. Many friends used to gather each morning at my uncle's shop, which was next to mine. They drank coffee, smoked, gossiped, swore, made rude jokes, cursed politicians and generally wasted time. But when Brother Anthoon was present, they were more restrained because they respected him. Brother Anthoon loved and followed Jesus passionately. He shared stories and recited verses from the Bible. He loved everyone and was kind to everyone. I looked forward to his visits.

One day, Brother Anthoon invited me to a service at his church. I accepted the invitation because it came from him. I did not know that this visit would change my life forever.

What I lacked most in my life then was what I most needed: peace. Real peace. The war had caused us so much pain – inner pain and turmoil. The preacher gave an invitation to follow Jesus. Although I was too shy to raise my hand, I opened my heart to Jesus. I put my trust in him, I asked him to forgive me and I decided to follow him entirely. I was seventeen years old. I left the service a different person, filled with joy and peace. I had never realized it before, but now I knew that this was what I had been longing for all my life. Without Christ, I was empty; with Christ, I had become a new creation.

I started to attend the church services regularly. I loved my new church family and I loved the world around me. I was filled with love for everyone. I would walk about looking at the people around me and smiling at them.

My friends noticed something different about me. I shared my story with them, and many came to faith as a result. Then I started to broaden my witness by learning to play the guitar. I often visited friends whom I knew from work with my guitar on my back. I had learned only a few chords, so I played most songs in A minor or E major! But it didn't matter. After playing and singing, I would preach – and my sermon was my testimony. Many were saved and are in my church today, and in other churches too.

My coming to faith also began another new chapter in my life. God instilled in me a deep desire to read and study. Although I longed to return to school, my job was too demanding and my family needed me. But I studied the Grade 9 to 12 textbooks during the evenings. At work, I read the Bible during my free time. I also began studying English at a language school.

At the age of twenty-one, I felt God's call into ministry. My pastor encouraged me to study theology. So I worked at my shop from early morning until just before 5:00 p.m., then studied at a local seminary from 5:00 p.m. until

9:00 p.m. At home, I did my homework, prepared for exams and looked after my sick father. I was also involved in ministry on the weekends – preaching and leading worship and youth services. I wanted to quit my studies a number of times, but my father's words kept coming back to me: "You are not a failure." The dean of the seminary was also a great source of encouragement. Four years later, I graduated first in my class. It was by God's grace and power that I was able to finish.

A year after graduation, I left for Prague to do a master's degree in theology. The first research paper I wrote was a disaster – I was told it was more like a sermon than an academic paper! But writing papers gradually became easier. I loved reading and spent all my free time in the library – I could not stop! However, I also had a job at the seminary, which involved cleaning toilets. I was so glad when I was promoted to cleaning the library! I learned a lot just by dusting the books on the shelves – I would take them down, read their titles and the names of the authors, and re-shelve them. Eventually, I would earn my master's degree with distinction.

Something else very important happened in Prague. It was there that I met Krista, the woman who became my dear wife. I know exactly when I first saw her. It was at 8:30 a.m. on 4 January 2002, and she was having breakfast before going home to Latvia after spending Christmas with friends in Prague. I knew I wanted to marry her – and she noticed me too. But she thought I might be a bit old for her, although I was only five years older than she was. I think living through the civil war accounted for my seeming much older.

Krista transformed my life. A year after we met, we were married in Prague. When I went to Latvia to meet her parents, her mother told me, "Krista is always right." We have joked a lot about this, but over the years I have discovered how right her mother was – Krista has been right in many things and I have learned a lot from her. She has been a great support in my ministry.

In 2004, I got a Langham scholarship and moved with my family to England to pursue a PhD at the University of Birmingham. I am very grateful to Paul Sanders (academic dean of the seminary where I studied in Lebanon) who recommended me for further studies. I have learned that you don't need many people to believe in you to help you succeed – one or two are enough.

In 2008, I finished my doctorate and Krista and I and our two children returned to Lebanon where I was appointed Academic Dean at the Arab Baptist Theological Seminary (ABTS). Soon I was also pastoring Hadath Baptist Church (now Resurrection Church Beirut), and over time this has become my primary role.

My personal journey – growing up during the civil war, studying and living abroad, being a husband and father – has helped me tremendously in leading and shepherding my church. Praise God that in his economy nothing is wasted. I am also very aware that I am where I am today because of the people who believed in me, and it is my desire to do the same for others, creating opportunities for them, especially if they are underprivileged.

A New Calling

In July 2008, my pastor, Ghassan Khalaf, a great man of God, a profound theologian, and a father figure for many, spoke to me. He had been at Resurrection Church Beirut (RCB) for over thirty years, but now he had an ardent desire to move from serving one local church to serving churches throughout the region. I knew his great abilities and assured him of my fullest support. Then he offered me the role of pastor of the church.

That evening, I shared his thoughts with my wife. After much prayer, we agreed to accept this responsibility, and two months later I took up my role as the pastor of RCB. At that time, it was a fairly typical Middle Eastern church, with an average attendance of about seventy people on Sunday mornings.

When I accepted the offer to pastor the church, I did so on one condition: I wanted to have the freedom to lead the church differently. I was unhappy with the typical Middle Eastern leadership model in which a father figure is at the top and all the other members of the family are below him. Both Krista and I felt that this leadership model was preventing the church from growing.

In August 2008, I met with the deacons of the church and shared my vision of a new leadership structure. They were welcoming and positive and we were all of one mind. We prayed as a team. I read a lot and worked very hard. I did some things right. I made some mistakes and learned from them. I read books on theology, on leadership, on management, on counselling and on spiritual formation. You can't lead a church well unless you are a man or woman of prayer, enjoy reading, and love people. Prayer moulds your character, reading sharpens your skills and expands your mind, and love transforms you and those you are working with.

In my first sermon, I asked that all the church ministries be put on hold and that the whole congregation come together, united in prayer to seek God's will for the church. Six weeks later, God drew our attention to the urgency of serving children rather than constructing our main worship hall.

So here's what I did very early on after becoming pastor:

- Heard God's voice through listening to the felt needs of the congregation.
- Cast the vision to everyone in the church, using various methods to communicate it.
- Empowered individuals to serve and lead according to their gifting. Having the "right people, in the right seat, on the right bus" was transformational. This included empowering women to serve and lead.
- Worked within a continuous cycle of structuring, reviewing and restructuring as the church grew.

Since then, the church has kept growing. Today, some nine years later, the church has 1,300 regular attendees across three campuses, and over two hundred life groups. The most significant statistic for this book, however, is that 70 percent of those attending are refugees.

3

Reaching

Shortly before the war began in Syria, God convicted us about the need to serve the marginalized. One of our church leaders visited Syrian workers in their homes. He loved them, ate with them, listened to their stories, and then prayed for them. Subsequently, he started a small group in his home. This touched their hearts deeply. Many, if not most, said to him, "No Lebanese have visited us and no one has ever invited us into their homes." In their homes, he used to pray and intercede for them, demonstrate love by investing his time and energy in them, and invite them back to his house for prayer, Bible study, and fellowship. This brought many to Christ. Thus in 2011, when the war in Syria broke out and Syrians started to flee to Lebanon, our church was somewhat prepared to receive them.

Visiting

When people in the West ask me, "What should we do to reach the refugees in our city?" I respond by asking, "Have you ever visited them in their homes?" Almost every time, the answer is no. This point was brought home to me again in early 2017 when I was in a taxi going to my hotel in Oslo after I had spoken at a Christian conference in Norway. As I was chatting with the Pakistani driver and telling him about the visions and dreams Arabs are receiving from God, I asked him if he had ever been visited by a Norwegian family. He said, "Never, they don't do that here."

Why not, I wonder? If we want to see God move in our life and the lives of others, we should, like our Master, meet our neighbors' families, especially the marginalized and the refugees among us. More than that, we should invite ourselves to their homes. I acknowledge that this is generally not the practice in Western cultures, where inviting oneself to another's home, especially where there is no established relationship, can be seen as intrusive. But few refugees will ever muster the courage to invite you to their home. I cannot emphasize enough what pride and pleasure it brings an Arab family to be able to host a guest or guests. It may feel uncomfortable and awkward for the Westerner, but you honor them by letting them become the hosts, letting them sit in the high place, while you learn how to be a guest in your own country, willing to sit uncomfortably, listen attentively and love abundantly.

This is the model Jesus himself used when he sent out his disciples, saying:

> The harvest is plentiful, but the laborers are few. Therefore pray earnestly to the Lord of the harvest to send out laborers into his harvest . . . Whatever house you enter, first say, "Peace be to this house!" And if a son of peace is there, your peace will rest upon him. But if not, it will return to you. And remain in the same house, eating and drinking what they provide, for the laborer deserves his wages. Do not go from house to house . . . eat what is set before you. Heal the sick in it and say to them, "The kingdom of God has come near to you." (Luke 10:2–9)

Listening

When you take the time to visit people, you should not be the one to do all the talking. It is not your job to instruct them on how to "fit in." Instead it is your job to listen – that is what we do when we love people. We seek to enter their worlds.

Some of this listening may be hard to do. Let me tell you some of the stories our church members have had to listen to: A woman told how she was forced to stand and watch as members of her family were sexually abused and killed in front of her eyes. She was told that if she showed any emotion or uttered a word, she too would be killed. Children have seen their parents die, and little girls have watched as men raped their mothers. One woman was fleeing with her daughter when a sniper shot the child. Another woman was carrying her three-year-old son when he was killed in her arms by a bullet. One woman's husband was killed in the war; another's stayed in Syria to fight. A woman told us that her cousin was slaughtered because of her faith. Her body was buried in front of her father's house so that everyone coming to visit would step on her as they entered the house. Some have seen heads impaled on the iron bars of balconies as a reminder of what happens to those who do not obey the ISIS regime, while others recall the headless bodies of women left hanging for days in public to instil fear of the authorities.

Iraqi and Syrian families have not only suffered these traumas, they have also endured the loss of their homes and all that they possess. Then, once they arrive in a host country, they may be treated very badly and endure more hardship. Some have been beaten in public, insulted, and taken advantage of. Those with higher education and degrees, who had good jobs in their home country, find themselves working as janitors, cleaners or laborers.

People have deceived one another and many have felt betrayed. Families who fled and trusted their friends to look after their homes discover that their friends have taken their property and sold their furniture.

As a result of these traumas, many people suffer from depression and live with a sense of loss. They live in fear of the future, in confusion and anxiety, feeling that the world has rejected them. Some have nightmares, others wake up screaming, some withdraw into loneliness, and others suffer selective mutism. Husbands become more aggressive with their wives and children, mothers scream and beat their children, and children and young people rebel.

Yet many churchgoers have no clue about the suffering that their Syrian or Iraqi neighbors have experienced. They may only have a vague idea about it because they have watched the news or a few YouTube videos. It is only as we sit with people (preferably in their own homes) that they will begin to trust us with their terrible memories.

Serving

Besides visiting and listening, there are many other ways in which we can serve refugees. Below are just a few ideas that we have tried. Use them to spark your own creativity.

Providing food and other supplies

Serve people by providing them with food. In one European country, a pastor from a Muslim background and I started a halal barbeque on the street in front of the church for the Yemenis in the community. We invited the local Pakistani butcher in his white gown to stand with us as we distributed kabab sandwiches. Hundreds of people came over and were extremely thankful for our generosity. This was an amazing way to connect with and witness to the neighborhood.

Refugees who have come to Lebanon and are not allowed to work for political and legal reasons greatly appreciate our practical love when we give them food parcels or food vouchers for use in a local supermarket. We find that the vouchers are always more welcome than the food parcels because they allow the family to choose what they want, within certain limits. One family told us that people had been bringing them bags of rice, so that they had huge amounts of rice but lacked almost everything else.

We can also serve people by providing medication, hygiene and winterization kits, milk and infant kits, school supplies and toys for children. By providing for refugees' basic practical needs, the church is protecting vulnerable people from turning to means that would bring shame to the family. We have been told that some mothers are willing to sell their bodies for as little as five dollars in order to get milk for their crying babies. The little we give saves the lives of many families and protects them from unethical practices and shameful acts.

Offering practical help

Refugees have practical needs that we can help them meet with the help of individuals and teams. For instance, we can help them paint their rooms and fix old equipment, provide transportation when they need to get somewhere, and help them to care for elderly family members.

Supporting education

Many refugee children are smart and want nothing more than to learn and study, but they just have no opportunity to do so. Paying their tuition fees is a priceless gift to these children. I well remember that when I was a child during the Lebanese civil war, my aunt used to pay for my school books. I am where I am today partially because of her generosity and love.

Refugee children do not lack the determination to become pastors, doctors, lawyers or entrepreneurs if they are only given the opportunity to get an education. But a lack of education could turn them into future terrorists. By showing them the love of Christ and giving them a good education, they have the potential to become the heroes of the Middle East.

Our church believes in the importance of education, especially early education. One of our leaders developed a program for at-risk Lebanese, Syrian and Iraqi refugees and migrant workers' children aged one to four. We also work with parents in an adult mentoring program that helps them develop the skills they need to create lasting, healthy and productive relationships with their children. We have an effective ministry among toddlers to help them develop musical skills and learn worship songs. We also have a supplementary program for children in school to help them with their studies, especially for those refugees who have come from Syria and are not familiar with the Lebanese educational system.

Marking life events

Refugees are cut off from their home communities. We can serve them by attending their weddings and burying those who die. You might be surprised to know that refugees do not have cemeteries. When their loved ones die, what do they do with their bodies? Where do they bury them? A number of years ago when we had just started to work with Syrian refugees, a Syrian woman died of cancer. When we offered to have her buried in our cemetery, our church experienced an amazing breakthrough. Her family and neighborhood were touched by how we honored the dead (and the living), and many conversions followed. Relationships became stronger and deeper. When people feel that you respect their dead as you do to the living, a deep bond is forged. They start to ask the most important question: "What makes you do this for our loved ones who have passed away?"

Incarnational Living

Being willing to humbly enter people's homes and listen to them is not just a psychological technique. It is a reflection of the nature of God. This is the point that the apostle Paul made in his letter to the Philippians. He urged the church members to practise humility in their relationships with one another, saying, "Do nothing from selfish ambition or conceit, but in humility count others more significant than yourselves" (Phil 2:3). He presented Christ as the supreme model of humble service in his incarnation, self-emptying, and willingness to become nothing, even a curse, in order to save those who are at enmity with God.

Many refugees feel (and are) rejected by those among whom they have come to live. They are despised or seen only as objects of charity. And that is how God could have related to us. He could have stayed proudly at a distance, dispensing advice about how we should live. But instead he came to live among us, sitting with people on the floor, sharing their food, listening to their stories and their struggles. He did not come to be served but to serve. Following Christ's example, one of our Lebanese pastors has refused to move to a more comfortable house and chooses instead to live among his Syrian brothers and sisters (who were once his enemies).

Christ's example of humility is our model. He entered into our world of despair and became what we cannot become in order to draw us to himself, reconciling us with God, and helping us to become like him. He entered into the experience of the human psyche and physical life without abandoning, contracting or diminishing his deity (John 1:1–18) and yet was still without sin (2 Cor 5:21; 1 Pet 2:22; Heb 4:15).

The church is called to the same self-emptying servanthood that aims to embrace and transform others. If we want to reflect God's character, we too have to be willing to move out of our comfortable way of life and go to those who are in need, not wait for them to come to us. As Louie Giglio has said, humility is the currency of the kingdom of God.

In our ministry among the refugees, we have discovered that humble service is transformational. Here I am not talking merely about food distribution but about a way of service that flows from the heart. I have seen a lot of food distribution that meets the physical needs of the body but is heartless and ignores the desperate cry of the soul. An incarnational life is an invitation into the life of others, an invitation to become for the other what he or she cannot be for themselves, and then an offer to embrace them in a way that helps them become the people God intended them to be.

How do we follow Jesus in his incarnation? We follow in the footsteps of Paul who said:

> Even though I am free of the demands and expectations of everyone, I have voluntarily become a servant to any and all in order to reach a wide range of people: religious, nonreligious, meticulous moralists, loose-living immoralists, the defeated, the demoralized – whoever. I didn't take on their way of life. I kept my bearings in Christ – but I entered their world and tried to experience things from their point of view. I've become just about every sort of servant there is in my attempts to lead those I meet into a God-saved life. I did all this because of the Message. I didn't just want to talk about it; I wanted to be *in* on it! (1 Cor 9:19–22 MSG).

4

Witnessing

We should be careful never to treat the people we meet merely as potential converts. They are people created in the image of God, and as such they deserve our love and care. But unfortunately, we sometimes go to the opposite extreme and fall prey to our own fears and do not share Christ with others. If it is true that 95 percent of believers in the world do not lead one person to Christ in their whole life, we are in serious trouble. This statistic would seem quite accurate, otherwise why would God have to visit people in dreams and visions if we were all sharing our testimony faithfully?

Our calling as believers is not merely to visit and to listen to others, it is also to speak in the way Paul encouraged when he said, "Let no corrupting talk come out of your mouths, but only such as is good for building up, as fits the occasion, that it may give grace to those who hear" (Eph 4:29). We should speak remembering that our Christian witness is a duty and a privilege. Christ has commanded us to do it, and by obeying his commandment, we receive the honor and the undeserved privilege of being part of his divine purpose

Telling Your Story

The best way to start a spiritual conversation is by sharing your story, and how your story plays its part in God's metanarrative. I have shared my conversion experience with many Muslim friends and strangers in the Arab world and in Europe, and not once do I remember any of them turning aggressive. People love to listen to stories, and personal stories are never threatening. It is when we are aggressive in our witness that people react badly.

I tell people that during the Lebanese civil war my father was sick and I had no peace. I was lost and in despair. I was working day and night to provide for my family. A friend of my father came to visit me in my shop. He was kind, and he shared his story with me. I became inquisitive and visited church with him. During the service God gripped my heart with such a message of love and peace that I responded by surrendering my life to Jesus. The peace I experienced was unexplainable and unbelievable. I tell them how I went to friends and relatives telling them about this amazing peace that filled my heart. I can still remember the love I experienced towards everyone – I was in love with Jesus and became in love with people, all people, even strangers walking past my shop. This peace, that I first experienced the night I gave my life to Jesus, is still present for me today, especially when I am deep in his presence.

That is my simple story; it is true for me and no one can take it away.

Listening to Their Story

In the Arab world, declaring one's faith by saying al-Shahada is foundational. People are accustomed to expressions of faith. Thus Christians should find it easy to share Christ boldly and with great confidence. The culture welcomes it. But it should be done with respect for the listeners.

Respecting the beliefs and value systems of others starts by listening attentively and wholeheartedly to their beliefs, faiths and convictions. People like to share about their own religion in the Arab world, and they also like to give their opinion about other religions. When we enter into dialogue with Muslims, they repeatedly speak about topics such as:

- The Qur'an being the final revelation of God to all and how God guarded it from error.
- That there is no God but Allah.
- The various articles of faith (including predestination and the day of judgement).
- The five pillars of Islam (*Shahadah* – the profession of faith; *Salat* – ritual prayers performed five times a day; *Zakat* – almsgiving; *Sawm* – fasting; and the *Hajj* – pilgrimage to Mecca).
- What Islam is and isn't, including the various meanings of *jihad*, the role of women, multiple marriages, good work, the afterlife, paradise and what is in it, and social, political and ethical issues.

It is very important that we allow Muslims to speak for themselves about their own faith and belief. Islam is not a monolithic religion, and people should be granted the right and freedom to speak for themselves about what they believe and why they believe it. Our job is to listen, to ask questions and certainly to challenge, but not to tell them what they believe.

Effective dialogue encourages all those who are present not just to listen but to respond, giving their own opinions and, when appropriate, proclaiming their faith. We see this in Christ's interactions with a Samaritan woman, a Jewish male leader (Nicodemus), a blind man, and many more. But Christ never left anyone at the same place where he first met them. Most dialogues led to a deeper encounter with him, a powerful proclamation of God's kingship and an open invitation to follow him.

Proclaiming Christ

Some of those who do not want to be perceived as aggressive in their witness jump to the other side of the spectrum and hide their lamp under a bowl. But freedom of belief should not lead us to withhold our witness; rather, freedom of belief should include the freedom to *share* our beliefs.

We do, however, need to make a clear distinction between aggressive evangelism and active and passionate evangelism. A passionate proclamation of the gospel bears long-term fruit; an aggressive approach creates division and animosity. Faithful Christians want the world to follow Jesus, but they will never use unethical means to achieve their goal or slander other people's faiths and beliefs, or deny their dignity. Deception, coercion, and abuse of power are all unacceptable methods of evangelism.

Effective proclamation in the Arab world takes place when we treat others with great respect and speak truth with love. It is love that brings people to Christ, and it is truth that keeps them in Christ. Our job is not to convert people, our job is to proclaim Jesus and invite people to follow him; it is the Spirit's job to convert people and transform their lives.

A good example of what this means is the apostle Paul's bold and passionate sharing of Christ with King Agrippa. After hearing Paul out, Agrippa responded, "In a short time would you persuade me to be a Christian?" And Paul said, "Whether short or long, I would to God that not only you but also all who hear me this day might become such as I am – except for these chains" (Acts 26:28–29). Paul's message was passionate and proclamational. People who speak like Paul are rising up in the Middle East and are leading many to follow Jesus.

Answering Their Questions

The apostle Peter said that we should be "prepared to make a defence to anyone who asks you for a reason for the hope that is in you; yet do it with gentleness and respect" (1 Pet 3:15). When Muslims ask us about the oneness of God, the Trinity, the corruption of the Scripture, the meaning of the Son of God, the prophethood of Muhammed, redemption and salvation, we should be ready to give answers. But our answers should be presented in gentle and respectful terms, for gentleness and respect are the vehicle that will carry our message when we defend the faith. Defending the faith should never include attacking other people's religions.

I once took a taxi to an airport in North Carolina, and the taxi driver happened to be Iranian. I introduced myself to him, and we had an interesting conversation. I asked him about his faith and I gave him the opportunity to share about his religion. He told me that he was not a very religious person. Then we had a conversation about whether someone should follow the teaching of Christ or of Muhammed. I asked the taxi driver to describe Muhammed to me and then I described Christ to him. At the end of the conversation, I asked, "Suppose you had been born in an atheist home, and that when you grew up you heard about Christ as revealed in the Bible and Muhammed the prophet of Islam, and you had to decide between the two of them. Who would you choose?" He replied that on the basis of what I had told him, he would follow Christ.

Of course, this kind of scenario is not typical, but the point I am making is that we can never enter into dialogue with someone like this taxi driver, or proclaim Christ, or defend what we believe without first respecting them as a person and their faith.

I think our church is able to serve and to witness powerfully in our region without much persecution because our Muslim friends know that we never treat them or their religion without respect and honor. The fact that this book can be written and published in the first place shows how much moderate Muslims respect us and honor the ministry we do. We are clear about our agenda: we want the whole world to follow Jesus; we want every person on earth to become a disciple of Jesus Christ. We don't hide our identity or our mission. We have never met, and I believe we will never meet, someone like Jesus. He is unique in his incarnation, life on earth, teaching, miracles, death on the cross, and resurrection. He has taken us to the top of the mountain into the presence of God. Before him came Moses and he took us midway towards the peak of the mountain. After Jesus, whoever comes can only take us back down. With Jesus, with his teaching and his life, we can reach the top of the mountain into the full presence of God. Christ is the beginning and the end.

The testimony of Nabeel Qureshi – who recently passed away, and to whom I pay tribute for his faithfulness and love for the Lord – was published in *Christianity Today* in February 2014. It is a powerful story of conversion involving a vision and three dreams that led him to Christ. But prior to this, Nabeel had a close relationship with a Christian friend called David who was instrumental in the unfolding of the story. Nabeel said:

> David didn't react like other Christians I had challenged. He did not waver in his witness, nor did he waver in his friendship with me. Far from it – he became even more engaged, answering the questions he could respond to, investigating the questions he couldn't respond to, and spending time with me through it all. Even though he was a Christian, his zeal for God was something I understood and respected. We quickly became best friends, signing up for events together, going to classes together, and studying for exams together. All the while we argued about the historical foundations of Christianity. Some classes we signed up for just to argue some more.[1]

David offers an example of what we should be doing as we reach out to our Muslim friends and neighbors.

Praying for God's Inviting

We can take courage from the fact that we are not acting alone when we ask people to believe in Jesus. God is at work before we are. He is the one who takes the initiative to draw people to Jesus. In the testimony above, David bore witness by trying to answer Nabeel's questions, but God was the one who ultimately drew Nabeel to himself through a vision and a dream. At other times, God uses visions and dreams to prompt someone to start seeking Christ, and we can help that person to start following Jesus.

For example, one Saturday after our evening service a woman asked me to pray for her because she wanted to follow Jesus. She told me she had been forced into marriage twice. Her second husband had seven marriages of convenience (a contractual marriage that lasts for only a short time) and she had been forced to serve each of his seven temporary brides. After having a dream about Jesus, she decided to run away and leave this life.

Others have had similar visions and dreams in which they see Jesus (or a spiritual being whom they identify as Jesus) inviting them to follow him. Some have told us about seeing crosses or Jesus on the cross, and some have spoken

---

1. www.christianitytoday.com/ct/2014/january-february/christ-called-me-off-minaret.html.

of seeing church buildings. Most of these dreams came at night, but we know of a few who have seen visions during the day. One man came to Christ after he saw a shining cross appear in the sky while he was walking along the street.

Some have had visions that resemble Bible stories. For example, one woman told us that after her husband had beaten her, she went to bed. In her dreams saw Jesus standing on the lake, inviting her to walk to him. In her dream she did that, and when she woke up she was full of joy and peace. This woman had never read the Bible and had never heard of Jesus's walking on water. She shared her story with one of our leaders, and she came to Christ when she discovered that Jesus had walked on water and had invited Peter to get out of the boat and walk towards him.

Another woman shared with us that she saw Jesus in a dream and went up to him. He showed her some words written on his thigh, "King of kings and Lord of lords." This woman had never read the book of Revelation, let alone Revelation 19:16 where Jesus is described in exactly the same way. On learning of this, and seeing the love of the church, she gave her life to Jesus.

Sometimes the vision is less explicit. For example, one Sunday morning a Syrian man from a non-Christian background attended church for the first time. My sermon was about "Jesus the Light of the World." As he listened, he remembered a dream about following the light that had haunted him for many years. He became convinced that the dream was being fulfilled and that it pointed to Jesus.

Many Arabs are choosing to follow Jesus nowadays. People are encountering him in visions and dreams. Some are seeking him because of a deep thirst and hunger for truth. Others are coming to him because of the love they see in the lives of their Christian friends. Others are experiencing deliverance, peace and freedom when someone prays for them in the name of Jesus. Still others are reacting to Islamic radicalization by seeking to become Christians. Our Christ is so unique and attractive that we cannot be silent or idle. People are coming to Christ from every direction. Even Jihadist leaders are being drawn to him. We are called to be proactive and invite the world to believe in Jesus, to put their trust in him, to change direction, and to follow him faithfully.

Conclusion

There is one final important point that needs to be made in this chapter: "Freedom of belief must include freedom of disbelief."[2] We need to remember

---

2. Kenneth Craig, *The Call of the Minaret* (Oxford: Oneworld, 2000), 307.

this when we invite people to come to Jesus. Brainwashing is not a virtue. Those who come to faith in Jesus should do so in response to an invitation, not coercion. And that invitation should be given in the context of loving, caring and giving that will continue even if our invitation to believe in and follow Jesus is rejected.

We must also be very clear that we do not want people to leave a religion to simply embrace another religion – we don't want Muslims to leave Islam and become religiously Christian; we don't want Muslims to abandon a system and get trapped in another system. We simply want all our brothers and sisters in the Arab world to follow Jesus, who is revealing himself to them in visions and dreams, through healing, and in the reading of Scripture. We believe that the restoration of the Arab world will happen when people choose to imitate Jesus fully and follow him regardless of the cost.

Muslims who visit our church do so voluntarily. When we provide food or medication, it is never on the condition that the recipients must attend our services. However, some choose to do so. When they – like so many others – get persecuted or forbidden to visit a church, they attend church from their own home. Today the Internet brings the world to us. Muslims around the world have unlimited access to church services in all languages. They watch, and they love to hear about Jesus, and many are choosing to follow and imitate him.

ONE TESTIMONY

On Sunday 22 November 2015, a gentleman from Sudan approached me after church, introduced himself as Brother Yassir. He mentioned the name of a common friend who had advised him to attend our church. I happened to be free for lunch, and so I invited him to join my family and a few friends at a nearby restaurant. Over the meal, he shared his story with us.

He came from a family of devout Sunni Muslims. One of his uncles played a major role in starting the Muslim Brotherhood in Sudan, and another was one of the top chiefs in the secret service in northern Sudan. When Yassir was only eight year's old, his father took him to a religious school far from his home and left him there. He did not know whether his father would ever return for him. For two years, Yassir attended that school, memorizing the Qur'an, and being radicalized by his Sunni teachers. Then his father showed up and took him home again.

Back home, Yassir attended the local school. There he met a Christian boy called Zachariah, who was the first in his class and used to sit next to him. Yassir regarded him as an infidel. So one day he and a friend took Zachariah into the forest and set about beating him to death. After breaking his bones, they left him there to die.

Yassir's family were also involved in persecuting Christians. In fact, one day, his uncle was sent to arrest a pastor. When he arrived at the church, he decided to wait until the service was over before making the arrest. Meanwhile the preacher, not knowing what was going to happen, was preaching from the book of Acts, telling the story of Saul's conversion. At the end of the service, Yassir's uncle went up to the pastor and asked him, "Why were you preaching about me and sharing my stories?" The pastor explained that he was telling a story from the Bible, but Yassir's uncle did not believe him until the pastor opened the book of Acts and read it to him. Yassir's uncle was captured by the power of the word of God and stayed until early the next morning asking the pastor questions. The conversation ended with Yassir's uncle giving his life to Jesus. His conversion, led to his being put in prison, yet there he was very active in evangelizing and many came to faith because of him.

One day, Yassir's cousin became very sick which led to his being admitted to hospital in a coma. His father could not go to him, for he was in prison, but he arranged for two Christian men to go to the hospital to pray for his son. The men arrived while Yassir was there, visiting his unconscious cousin. Yassir watched as the two messengers went inside to pray for the boy. When they had finished praying, he saw the boy open his eyes, start to remove all the tubes attached to him, and on the same day the boy was healed and went out to play. Yassir was dumbstruck. How could the prayers of two infidels be heard by God, and how come God responded by granting them a miracle? He decided that he needed to learn more about Christianity. He went home and started to read once again all that was written about Jesus in the Qur'an and in Islamic traditions.

To cut a long story short, Yassir ended up giving his life to Jesus. As a result, his family disowned and abandoned him. More than that, they went to a graveyard and put his name on a grave as a sign that he was dead to them. Rejected and persecuted, Yassir decided to leave Sudan. Before leaving, he went and stood by his "grave" and wept and wept. He loved his parents and was in agony that they had rejected him. It was the darkest moment in his entire life.

As he was standing there, he felt a hand touching his shoulder and a voice said, "Yassir, don't cry; your grave is empty and so is mine." He felt God's amazing presence, and a calling from God to go and serve him and witness to the resurrection. He left Sudan, continued his studies in Islamic Studies and Jurisprudence, and earned an MA from Columbia International University. Today he is a lecturer and pastor of migrant Churches in Germany. Recently he published his autobiography in German (see, Yassir Eric, *Hass gelernt, Liebe erfahren: Vom Islamisten zum Brückenbauer*, Asslar adeo, 2017; see also his testimony on Youtube: https://youtu.be/ydQyPYTRi3I).

Twenty-five years later, Yassir visited Egypt to teach at a pastors' conference. While speaking and sharing his testimony, he noticed that one pastor with a broken arm and a broken leg was in tears. After Yassir was finished, he went to this pastor and asked him why he had been weeping. The pastor, blind in one eye and physically fragile, told him, "I am Zachariah, the little boy you beat twenty-five years ago." Then Zachariah opened his Bible, and there on the first page of his Bible was the name of Yassir, written by the hand of the Christian teenager he had tried to kill. Zachariah said, "Since that day, I have not stopped praying for you. It is wonderful to know that you are a follower of Jesus." Yassir himself was in tears now. As he stood in front of Zachariah and saw what the beating had done to him, and saw also his loving heart, he could only ask, "What kind of religion can make one love an enemy so much!"

We should invite others to make the same commitment, even if it comes at great cost. If there is one person worth trusting in the world, it is Jesus. Those who follow in his footsteps will find their lives more meaningful and will see others blessed as they walk behind the one who gave his life to give us fullness of life.

5

Changing

At this stage, you might expect me to launch into a discussion of how to disciple Muslims and other refugees who turn to Christ. I know that this is a vital concern. It is at the heart of my ministry. But before we can go there, there is another point that I need to make. It is that we must not forget that the gospel (the good news) transcends both the preacher and the person preached to. In other words, both the evangelist and the listener are changed and transformed by the power of the word of God.

The story of the conversion of the house of Cornelius (a Gentile centurion) in Acts 10 is too well known to need to be repeated here fully. A key point in that story is that it was not just Cornelius who was converted. Peter's vision from God led him also to a different kind of conversion. This "second conversion" (to embrace Gentiles as fellow Christians) was necessary in order for Peter to lead Cornelius to faith. Sometimes we too need a second conversion before we can embrace and welcome in those we think of as outsiders.

Transformation is always a two-way street; it never goes just one way. I can confidently say that we were transformed by the refugees as much as they were transformed by the message of the gospel and the work of the church.

Transforming Leadership

When you think about it, it is not surprising that Peter was the one who had to be transformed first. He was the leader of the apostles, and once he was convinced of the need to reach out to Gentiles, others would follow. In the same way, it was one of our church leaders who took it upon himself to visit refugees who opened the door for our wider ministry.

If you want your local church to minister to refugees, your pastor and church leaders should have a holistic vision of ministry. They need to recognize that the church does not exist only to call people to repentance, nor is its aim simply to send people to heaven. The church as a faithful new creation has the role of transforming the community by being conformed to the likeness of Jesus and by collectively imitating him on a daily basis.

Moreover, the leadership of the church should create a culture of generosity, taking the lead on giving abundantly to the mission of the church and serving the community. If you are not showing the way, the people will not follow. It all starts at the top.

Transforming the Leadership Team

Sometimes pastors complain to me that although they wish to broaden their ministry, their congregations are not embracing different ethnic groups within the church. My question to them is always, are people from other ethnic groups embraced on the leadership team? If your church in England or Germany or Sweden wants to reach out to refugee communities, are you willing to invite refugee believers and emerging leaders onto the leadership team? Ethnic divisions within the congregation are far more easily addressed when the leaders model unity, trust and collaboration in a multi-ethnic team.

The above statement may seem like common sense, but it is surprising how seldom churches recognize that to serve a multi-ethnic congregation, they need a multi-ethnic leadership team. At RCB, for example, our leadership team now includes Lebanese, Syrians, Egyptians, Iraqis, and a few expatriates. This has come about because early in our ministry at RCB, I realized that we were relying on Lebanese leaders to make decisions on behalf of all the ethnic groups in the church. Not only did this create the impression that the Lebanese were the natural leaders, but it also resulted in other groups being misrepresented and neglected as we inevitably approached issues from the perspective of the Lebanese community. But we discovered that refugees and displaced people have different spiritual needs that need to be reflected in our preaching, different physical needs that need to be included in the church budget, different relational needs that result in a greater emphasis on life groups, and different social needs, with different feast days and occasions for celebration. It was only when we empowered leaders from these communities that RCB learned how to meet these needs properly. At the same time, the leaders from the different ethnic groups helped us to see the strengths (and not merely the weaknesses) in their communities and traditions.

It would be sad if some churches had their core leadership teams made up from the same ethnic background, while the congregation itself is multi-ethnic. This situation may reflect mistrust of others, a desire for control, or the belief that because a specific ethnic group has been around for a while "they know what is best for the whole church".

How does one go about creating a multi-ethnic leadership team? The first step is to preach and teach about the importance of a biblically sound leadership model that breaks down racial barriers on the leadership level and faithfully represents the needs of a multi-ethnic congregation. Such preaching flows easily from the book of Acts. There we learn that the church was born on the day of Pentecost when Peter preached his first sermon, and about three thousand were baptized (Acts 2). Thereafter the church grew and grew – and so it attracted attention and persecution. As a result, the believers "were all scattered throughout the regions of Judea and Samaria" (Acts 8:1).

Some of those who fled the persecution made their way to Antioch in the Roman province of Syria (not far from modern Lebanon) and planted a church there that included both Jews and non-Jews (Acts 11:19–21). When the church leaders in Jerusalem heard about this, they sent Barnabas to Antioch to find out more about what was happening there. He saw that God was at work and that his own job was to encourage and strengthen the believers by urging them to remain faithful to Christ (Acts 11:22–23). Under his leadership, the church in Antioch retained close ties to its mother church. When an economic crisis loomed in Judea, the Christian believers in Antioch sent money to help their Christian brothers and sisters there (Acts 11:29).

Barnabas was by no means the only leader of the church in Antioch. His fellow leaders included "Simeon who was called Niger, Lucius of Cyrene, Manaen a lifelong friend of Herod the tetrarch, and Saul" (Acts 13:1). Their names tell us that this was a diverse, multi-ethnic leadership team.

The believers at Antioch were so committed to Christ that their non-believing neighbors started to refer to them as "Christ-ians." They were also devoted to mission and to seeking the leading of the Holy Spirit. It was while they were worshiping and fasting that the Holy Spirit instructed them to send Barnabas and Saul out as missionaries (Acts 13:2). Later, Barnabas and Paul returned to this church and reported on "all that God had done with them, and how he had opened a door of faith to the Gentiles" (Acts 14:27). When this welcoming of non-Jews into the church became a source of controversy, the issue was discussed at length with the mother church in Jerusalem (Acts 15:1–35).

But preaching on Acts and other passages is not enough. We must also model leadership by encouraging every mature leader, starting with the pastor, to mentor a potential leader from a different ethnic group. So a few years ago we made it our official policy that every leader at RCB should have an emerging leader from a different background shadowing him or her in their ministries. The leaders took this seriously. Marie, one of our younger leaders, eventually earned the nickname "Duck" because she was always accompanied by a flock of ten or twelve "ducklings." When my wife and I invited her for lunch one Sunday after church, she came on a bus with fourteen emerging female leaders. Instead of serving one, we had the privilege of serving fifteen!

In our annual conference, we intentionally ask Syrian and Iraqi leaders to lead Lebanese discussion sessions and small groups. Our humanitarian aid manager who serves the Syrian community is Iraqi, and some Iraqi groups are led by Lebanese leaders. Our leadership model of engaging different ethnic groups in ministry is a lived culture rather than just a course we offer from time to time. Thus at RCB, many followers of Jesus from non-Christian backgrounds are either life group leaders or leading other ministries. Their faithfulness to the gospel, their servant hearts and their leadership skills bring them trust, acceptance and authority in the church. Just recently, we asked a Syrian follower of Jesus to lead a Lebanese Bible study group – he did an outstanding job, and great feedback was received from his group, while he himself greatly enjoyed it.

Naturally, you may find that people gravitate to life groups led by people of their own ethnicity. This is not wrong, as such leaders can understand the hearts of their people. But it can have the unfortunate side effect of creating ethnic ministry silos, with groups operating in parallel but never interacting. This type of grouping can spread distrust of other groups, and over time it can result in church splits. So it is important that leaders from across the ethnic divide meet at training sessions and seminars where they have an opportunity to connect at a deeper level, grow in their trust of one another, and learn to collaborate in their various ministries.

Transforming the Congregation

Do not make the mistake of assuming that this transformation will be easy. At RCB we found that when the Syrian refugees first started arriving in Lebanon, the congregation and many of our leaders were annoyed and even hostile to them. They accused the Syrians of spying, of coming only to get food or money, and of pretending to become Christian because they thought it would make it easier for them to get visas to other countries. These were valid concerns. In fact, many refugees have publicly shared that these were indeed their initial motives in coming to us. But when people experience the love of Christ in practical ways, in addition to encountering the word of God and the Spirit of

God, they often change. Now many of these people willingly share food parcels they receive with others who are in greater need.

Some parents also objected when we began loving, serving and inviting Syrians to our church. They said things like "We don't want our kids to play with their kids"; "I don't feel comfortable sitting next to them"; "I don't like their smell"; "I don't want to go to the same restrooms as them"; "I am no longer comfortable at church"; "I come here and I feel like a stranger and that everyone is looking at me." What is a pastor to do when such emotions are expressed?

The first thing to do is to recognize that people are different. The leaders should take the lead in welcoming newcomers, but we should not expect everyone else to get on board straightaway. Some people need more time to adapt than others. They should not be made to feel inferior or unwanted or be forced to suppress their concerns. There should be a safe place for them to express these concerns without feeling judged by others. We should listen to their fears and acknowledge them, for when people know that they are being heard, they are more likely to be willing to change.

While listening to the reluctant, the leaders should stay focused on the church's vision and continue to communicate it on a regular basis. We found that all leaders had to work at showing the same affection to Syrians and Iraqis as they show to Lebanese. Leaders are always watched, and if they show any favouritism, it will be sensed by the congregation. When individuals see how their leaders are showing affection to others, they will follow their lead.

One very effective technique for bringing people together is to ask people to give their testimonies. When, for example, the Lebanese hear the testimonies of Syrians or Iraqis during a service or other gathering, they are convinced of the genuineness of their faith and this builds a spiritual bond and develops trust.

Transforming Our Style of Worship

In his incarnation, Jesus became like us, flesh and blood, and moved into our neighborhood. This also means that he physically looked like us. He most likely had black not blond hair, brown not green or blue eyes, a Levantine-size noise (a bit bigger than yours!), darker skin, and would have dressed like a typical first-century Jewish man. He resembled the men of his time. The church should follow Jesus's model of integration in order not to look bizarre to its community and be rejected.

Yet as a consequence of missionaries coming to the Arab world in the mid-twentieth century, most evangelical churches in Lebanon today look like mid-1950s buildings in the USA and nothing like the historic Catholic and

Orthodox churches of the Middle East. Yet if you look at mosques in the Arab world today, they look similar to the old Orthodox churches and cathedrals, mainly because centuries ago Arab invaders built their mosques on the pattern of the local churches, hiring local Christians to plan and build them, or in many cases, taking over church buildings and turning them into mosques. Church planters today could do well to follow their example – not by invading and taking over other people's religious properties but by learning about and preserving cultural norms and aesthetic shapes and structure as a vehicle for carrying the word of the kingdom. I am pretty sure that this is acceptable in the twenty-first century.

However, in practice, things are more complicated. Let me explain: The church that I am pastoring today is fifty years old. It started with a few Palestinian families, some Lebanese and a few expatriates. When I was invited to pastor it in 2008, it looked like a typical Southern Baptist Church of the 1970s or 1980s. Today, we have become rather like a contemporary evangelical church in the West and our lively worship team is inspired by Hillsong and other worship bands. I am fully aware that this style is far removed from typical Arab thinking and styles, but many love it. And as more and more people from non-Christian backgrounds are joining the church, we are increasingly mixing musical styles, developing local worship songs, and bringing in different musical instruments. The clash of two cultures within one setting has created a third culture that we all enjoy.

Some people ask, why not drop the Western style and keep the Arab style? The first answer is because media are bringing the whole world together, and the average Arab young person listens to Western songs, watches Western movies, plays Western games, and spends more time on social media than on watching Arabic movies or listening to Arabic songs. If we were to adopt only the style of the local culture, we would lose all the young men and women who have a global Western culture. The second reason we don't drop the imported way of doing worship is because the older members from a Christian background enjoy it immensely. Finally, members of the historic churches in the Arab world (Catholic, Orthodox, Maronite, etc.) and educated open-minded Muslims in our communities also enjoy our style of worship. When Hillsong UK had a concert in Lebanon on 31 August 2017, the venue was packed with teenagers and young adults from evangelical, charismatic, Catholic, Orthodox and non-Christian backgrounds. The reality that we need to acknowledge is that contemporary Western worship is bringing people together in the Arab world. We have blended different styles that our congregation find creative and necessary.

Our life groups give individuals the freedom to join a group of their preference (as regards culture, worship style, etc.), but in our congregational worship we integrate all these different pieces into an artistic mosaic. The congregation know that when we all come together, all styles are welcomed and integrated: local and Western music, songs in Arabic, English or Spanish, sitting on a chair or on the floor, having the sermon preached while standing or while sitting. They also know that there is no one dress code for everyone (more on this in a later chapter).

As for the structure of our buildings, this is also challenging nowadays. If churches have the financial resources, they can choose between erecting a structure modelled on a historic church, a local mosque, or a sophisticated contemporary worship center. Some turn an apartment into a local church and have their worship services there. (Note that we do not encourage this unless they have no other option.) Whatever option is chosen, some will not like it. Our research showed that the younger generation did not care for traditional buildings, and so we, as a church, decided to be forward-looking and invest in and attract the next generation.

On another note, we have resisted the trend that encourages non-Christian background believers to have their own worship centers separate from believers from a Christian background. We found this to be unbiblical and dangerous, for it only encourages further segregation. From its very outset, the church has been and is a variety of peoples and cultures that reflects the very nature of the kingdom of God. So on the one hand, we make an extra effort to celebrate together as one diverse church, but on the other hand we respect people's cultural identity and encourage them to be part of life groups in order to practise and live out their faith in a way that is appropriate in their own culture.

Conclusion

Above all, we are to be sensitive to the voice of the Spirit, just as the church in Antioch was when it set Paul and Barnabas apart for a new ministry (Acts 13:2). The Spirit reveals God's agenda, appoints those who will carry out God's mission, and anoints them to execute it. The church's role is not to write the agenda, but to execute *God's* agenda. We do this by following the wind of the Spirit.

A few years ago, a group of leaders in our church wanted to start a ministry to reach out to a certain group of young men in a particular part of Beirut. Thankfully, we did not do it, nor put our resources behind it. Instead, we moved towards where God was moving. Muslims were, and still are, seeing dreams and visions, and Syrians and Iraqis were so thirsty for the gospel. So, we followed the wind.

It is said that "when the wind of change blows, some build walls while others build windmills." We don't want to be a church that builds walls when the wind of God sweeps throughout the Middle East. Some churches, however, have redefined their calling and clearly stated that their ministry is focused solely on Lebanese Christians. The challenge is if some churches can not make up their minds whether or not to serve the huge waves of Syrian refugees coming into the country. However, by being indecisive, they have indirectly already made the decision to pass up the opportunity. No decision is nonetheless a decision, and that comes with its own consequences. At RCB, we were one of the few churches who built windmills and were carried with the wind, sowing the seeds of total surrender and reaping the fruits of God's immeasurable blessings.

6

Nurturing

Unfortunately, some Christian agencies are primarily interested in the number of people who make a public or private decision to follow Jesus and have little interest in discipling new followers of Jesus. Researchers who have investigated their claims about the number of Muslim converts say that up to 90 percent of these converts revert to Islam. This finding may be correct in some situations. For example, sometimes people are asked to "raise their hands" to signal their commitment to Jesus and are then counted as new converts. But they may simply have raised their hands because the preacher persisted in calling for people to raise their hands so that the number of hands could be counted in photos of the event that could be shared with donors. Meanwhile, the people themselves either did not understand that their action would be seen as a commitment to Christ, or were hoping for some personal benefit in the form of food parcels or financial aid, or were reacting emotionally along with the rest of the crowd.

I am convinced that most respected pastors do not fall into this trap. We are in the business not only of calling people to Jesus but also of making disciples. The quality of people is even more important than the quantity. Admittedly, we have all made mistakes in the past, and even here at RCB some new followers of Jesus were not shepherded as they should have been; there is no doubt that some have reverted to Islam. One major reason this has happened is that we have not always taken discipleship seriously enough. It is also true that some of the existing discipleship tools are ineffective because they are merely translations of Western books that do not speak to our own culture and acknowledge our present realities. That is why we have developed our own course, which we call the pathway to discipleship (for more details on this course, see the Appendix). The key point that I want to emphasize here is that the church is, and should always be, absorbed in promoting lifelong discipleship.

So in this chapter I will talk about how we relate to those who express an interest in turning to Christ, and in later chapters I will talk about how we encourage them to grow and mature as disciples.

Believing in Jesus

Let's begin by spelling out the four things we are asking all people, whatever their background, to do when we ask them to believe in Jesus:

Trust him

Believing is not just a state of mind; it is a deliberate decision to trust in Jesus Christ as the one who is indeed the way to the Father. It involves trusting that he is the Way, the Truth, and the Life eternal, and that he can give us fullness of life, enabling us to experience the life of God in us, through us and around us. Believing means trusting that he is our Savior and Redeemer, and that he meant it when he said, "the Son of Man did not come to be served, but to serve, and to give his life a ransom for many" (Mark 10:45). It is trusting that if we follow him, this will be good for us, good for our community, and good for the world because he is indeed the best teacher and the Savior of the world.

Repent

Trusting in Jesus Christ results in a change in the way we live. We change direction. Instead of going our own way, we follow his way. Repenting involves asking him to forgive our rebellious past, our slowness to recognize him, and all the times we took a path that was not the path he wanted us to be on. It involves acknowledging that our sins have broken his heart and caused pain to others.

Follow in his footsteps

In Arabic, as well as in Greek and other languages, the words for believing (having faith) and being faithful come from the same root. When we put our faith in Jesus, we start following him, just as disciples used to follow and obey their teachers. Because we have trusted in Jesus, we walk just behind him. We do good deeds not because we need to earn our salvation but because we are already saved and are following our Savior.

Crown him as king

When we come to Jesus, we do so because of who he is, and not for what we can get from him. We acknowledge him as our Savior, but we also worship him as our Lord. He is the ruler of the universe, the King of kings and Lord of lords, and so we too must crown him king over every aspect of our lives. We must seek his way and not ours in our personal life, in our marriage, in our ministry and in the workplace.

Walking Alongside

As we all know, agreeing to do those things is one thing; following through is another. Discipleship does not happen in an instant but is a lifelong process.

Based on our own experiences at RCB, both successes and failures, we now propose a pathway for effective discipleship. This pathway takes seriously the teaching of the Gospels as a foundation for Christian discipleship, guiding and supporting those who sincerely believe in Christ and are filled with his Spirit. It is not to be looked upon as a program but as a lifestyle. Discipleship does not consist primarily of learning doctrine; rather, it involves a deep transformation, from the inside out, of the whole person – mind, body, soul and spirit.

Our model, once again, is drawn from the life of Jesus. Like him, we seek to nurture discipleship by entering into a deep relationship with those who have become disciples. When he became incarnate, he did not only invite himself into our world; he also invited us into his world and into his presence. That is why Mark's gospel constantly speaks of his calling people to him and sending them out to call others to him.

What this means for us as disciples is that we are called to follow Jesus and to invite apprentices to follow us. In this context, the apprentices are new believers whom we are to invite to follow us so that they may observe, learn and then be sent to do the same. The simple (but rarely practised) principle is that every disciple should have both a teacher and an apprentice.

There are good scriptural grounds for inviting people to follow Jesus alongside us and imitate us in our walk with Jesus. Hebrews 13:7 says, "Remember those who led you, who spoke the word of God to you; and considering the result of their conduct, imitate their faith" (NASB). In 2 Thessalonians 3:7, Paul says, "For you yourselves know how you ought to follow our example, because we did not act in an undisciplined manner among you" (NASB), and also in 1 Corinthians 11:1 he says, "Be imitators of me, just as I am also of Christ" (NASB). In Philippians 4:9, Paul strongly states "the things you have learned and received and heard and seen in me, practise these things; and the God of peace shall be with you" (NASB).

Just as a child needs an adult to imitate in order to grow to maturity, so people need an example to imitate if they are to grow to maturity. We should invite new followers to walk alongside us as we grow spiritually and serve our world. New believers need to see our teaching expressed in our daily living, through our character and actions. We need to invite them to see how we call people to follow Jesus, how we teach, set free, heal and pray for others and for ourselves. We need to model Christ for them through close and loving relationships that are intentional, which will help them to imitate Christ as they see Christ in the lives of his disciples.

It is not enough in the Arab world to merely preach to people. New believers need to see (not only hear about) this new way of life in Jesus. They have only been exposed to one way of life and to one style of living, and they need to see a different lifestyle in order for them to understand it and be fully transformed.

Yet the problem is that leaders around the globe are too busy to walk alongside new believers; teachers at seminaries are too overloaded to invest in the life of their students outside of class; pastors in churches can barely balance their lives and ministry with the growing demands of their congregations. So how are we to address this need for connection? The only way is through effective life group ministry in the church. That is why we have over two hundred life groups at RCB in which we help believers connect not just with individuals but with a group. These life groups form spontaneously as individuals invite their friends and relatives to come to the life group they attend. When such groups grow too large for one leader to mentor, or too large for the place where they meet, we encourage them to split into two groups. However, we also arrange special events at which newcomers to the church and people we have met through our work in the community can get to know each other and can be connected in new life groups.

Belonging to a life group is one way of acknowledging that Jesus is Lord over our relationships. As followers of Jesus, we want all our relationships to be holy. We want our family relationships to honor God. We want our friends to know Christ and become his disciples. And we want to be friends with those who also worship him so that we can encourage and learn from each other what the lordship of Christ means in regard to our relationships. This is what life groups do as they share life together, shepherd one another, pray for one another, and grow together.

Yasser, a Syrian follower of Jesus, tells story after story of how his life group leader, Majdi, is always ready to serve and help him. When he is in trouble, Yasser knows he can call his brother-in-Christ, who will always be there to stand by him and help – no matter what, where or when. Hulia, another Syrian refugee, came to Lebanon in 2012 and met Jesus through the church. She is still a faithful follower of Jesus although she now lives in Sweden. She has told us on several occasions that what drew her to Christ was the servant heart and unconditional love of the leaders she met:

> What drew me to Christ is your love, your welcome and hospitality, and your serving heart. Even though we have different ethnic and religious backgrounds, you loved us and served us in a way that our own people did not even think of doing. I remember how some of the church leaders came over, knocked on our door, and asked whether we needed anything and expressed their readiness to serve us. When we were in pain you were next to us, and when we were happy you were also happy with us. You have become our family. Even after we had left for Norway, you kept asking after us. We love our church and we continue to follow your services online.

The relational dynamic helps the new follower of Jesus to see a living model of the living Christ among us. It also encourages the mentor (or life group leader) to live in daily imitation of Christ.

It might not be going too far if I said that most, if not all, of those who choose to follow Jesus continue to do so because of their close relationships with faithful followers of Jesus, who themselves observed their leaders' behavior and imitated them, so that they in turn grew into maturity and leadership. When we hear stories of people reverting to Islam, it is often because they reacted enthusiastically or emotionally to the message of the gospel but were not followed up with close relationships and good training in discipleship. The seed that was planted died because it was left alone in the scorching sun.

As new believers walk alongside us, they observe our spiritual and prayerful lives and they go and do likewise. In the context of discipleship as a true encounter with God in Christ whom we follow, the spiritual dynamic involves building a growing relationship with the Master through being spiritually in his presence and through an ongoing conversation.

Karen, a friend of mine from California, once told me, "You can't be in God's presence unless you are in the present." Often, we either live in the past or in the future and miss enjoying God's presence in the present. The present was the future of yesterday and will be the past of tomorrow. We want our disciples to see us live in the present and in his presence. The spiritual dynamic will help followers of Jesus to be in harmony with Christ and thus meet their inner needs and desires. We need to draw alongside them so that they may experience our inner peace, hear how God loves us and forgives us, see how we receive spiritual guidance, battle temptation and overcome fear, loneliness, disappointment and bondage – and in turn learn to grow in the knowledge of these truths and in our understanding of God the Father, Son and Holy Spirit, and of what Christ has done for us through his incarnation, perfect life, death, and resurrection.

Sending Out New Followers

Finally, we send new followers out to do the same things we have been doing. As they go to make disciples, their character develops and grows to become more and more in harmony with the image of God in them. Their soul, character, mind, thinking, belief, attitudes, habits, actions, emotions and behavior will be joined together into a humanity that reflects the very nature of Jesus, who came to teach us how to be truly human.

Our disciples are not to stay with us but to go to the world and do as we have done (at the least) or as Jesus did (at the most). We encourage them to call other people to follow Jesus, to teach the ways of the kingdom, to free people from bondage, to heal the sick, and to set aside time for prayer and spiritual disciplines.

One day, two women came to see me. One of them told me that when one of our pastors had prayed for her to become pregnant after many years of barrenness, God had answered immediately and within a few months she was pregnant. She asked me to pray that her friend too might fall pregnant. But instead of my praying for her friend, I asked her to turn to her friend and do the same as the pastor had done for her. And so she prayed for her friend and I joined them.

Another example: a child had food poisoning but his mother could not take him to hospital. She contacted her life group leader to ask him to come and pray for the child, but he was not available. Then she took the initiative and prayed herself – her son instantly improved.

At RCB, leaders know that they are not permitted to lead any ministry without empowering others and investing in others. Everyone should be equipping someone to take his or her place. Sending our disciples to do the same is mandatory for the expansion of the kingdom.

We believers from a Christian background should trust the followers of Jesus from non-Christian backgrounds and give them space to lead and to serve. One day the war in Syria will end, as well as the war in Iraq. People will eventually return home or settle in a different country. We want them to be well equipped as disciples of Jesus to plant churches – even if they don't have buildings – and to multiply – even if they don't have resources. The word of God will sustain them. The Spirit will lead them to crown Christ as Lord in their lives. The communities they will develop will keep them strong. Their witness will attract many to Christ, and as they make disciples, Christ's kingdom will expand and the Father will be glorified and communities restored.

7

Teaching and Instructing

Jesus not only embodied, coached and mentored the ways of the kingdom, he taught the ways of the kingdom through sermons and parables. He proclaimed the good news and invited people to repentance. The Sermon on the Mount offers a summary of what he taught his disciples and the crowd that gathered around him. He also taught through parables. In private, Jesus instructed the disciples, rebuked them for their lack of faith, and encouraged and empowered them to go and preach the gospel.

We are all grateful for his teaching, and we all know the importance of teaching, but how intentional are we in teaching believers? We live at a time when mentoring, counselling and coaching prevail over teaching. Do not misunderstand me, I do believe there is place for all these approaches and leaders should be practising all of them: mentors want to help their mentees draw from their (the mentor's) own experiences; coaches want to push the person, drawing from their (the coachee's) own resources and experiences; and the counsellor wants to diagnose a client's psychological and emotional state in order to help him or her get well. But I am wary when leaders tend to only use one model and reject the others.

We live in an age where we can't tell people directly what they are supposed to do, especially in spiritual and ethical matters. I am all for drawing from people's experience, I am all for pushing my students to set their own goals and take action to solve their own problems, I am all for becoming a professional coach where we give "little advice and make few suggestions" in order to push people to think for themselves and take responsibility. But occasionally, as Spirit-filled and Spirit-led leaders, we need to take action and tell people what they should be doing.

Teaching like Jesus

Jesus is our model for how we should teach, and the Middle East and North Africa need this model more than any time before. In Matthew 19:16–22, Jesus, who could see into the heart, spoke frankly with a rich young man and told him clearly what he was to do: "If you would be perfect, go, sell what you possess and give to the poor, and you will have treasure in heaven; and come, follow me." That is quite a powerful statement. There are also hundreds of other references in the Gospels to Jesus teaching through giving clear commandments (Matt 5–7; Matt 28:18–20; Mark 5:19; 9:39; 10:11–12; Luke 13:2–3; 17:20; 21:34–37; John 3:3–13; 4:13–14, 16, 21–24; 12:7; 21:15–23). Because this book you are reading is about imitating Jesus and creating disciples, we cannot ignore this dimension of Jesus's life.

Jesus taught not only through words but also symbolically through his actions; actions that carried a message. For example, when he cleared out the temple (Mark 11:15–18), he was symbolically enacting the destruction of the temple, and revealing his Messiahship and royal role. In Mark 11:1–11, he deliberately entered Jerusalem riding on a donkey, a symbolic action that clearly echoed Zechariah 9:9–10 and staked a royal claim. On another occasion, Jesus took a child in his arms and taught a lesson about accepting little ones (Mark 9:36–37). In Mark 2:15–16, Jesus ate with sinners and tax collectors, revealing the heart of our Father in heaven and showing that, through the coming of Jesus, sinners are privileged guests of God. The miracles in the Gospels are not merely "wonder stories" or occasional works of charity; they are also signs (or symbolic acts) that carry deeper meaning. They reveal new teachings about the kingdom of God, the Messiah and discipleship.

It is thus safe to say that imitating Jesus requires both bold teaching and intentional actions. In a discussion with a Muslim friend who lives in the UK, he told me that his relatives and friends have little respect for Christian leaders. They find them weak, indecisive, shaky and uncertain; whereas Jesus in his teaching by word and deed was daring, courageous, brave and fearless. To be courageous does not mean to be polemic and attack other faiths (though this method is being used and has its pros and cons); it means proclaiming Christ boldly yet lovingly, using confident rhetoric accompanied by a transformational way of life and radical deeds of love that witness to the power of the words spoken. Followers of Jesus should be exhorted to imitate Jesus by teaching the ways of the kingdom through powerful words and deeds.

One final point we should note about Jesus's parables and stories is that he drew them from the context in which he lived and told them using everyday language that was accessible to his listeners. Sadly, a lot of the Christian books we read in the Middle East or the Christian TV programs we listen to are translated from other languages. For example, a Kurdish Christian leader once told me about a Christian organization that received a large sum of money to translate material from Portuguese into Kurdish. They hired translators to translate the material from Portuguese into English, then from English into Arabic, and from Arabic to Kurdish. How much was lost in this long chain of translation, I wonder? How contextualized was the final product? The person who did the translation from Arabic to Kurdish told me that he had to amend a lot of his text because the prosperity teaching it contained was unrealistic and unknown to Kurdish refugees who have no home, no permanent shelter, no mattresses to sleep on, and yet are willing to follow Jesus and carry the cross on a daily basis.

The Content of Our Teaching

When it comes to the content of our teaching, one of the points our church stresses over and over again is that the word of God (in the Old and New Testament) is our canon (literally, our "measurement tool") and our reference point for our worship, conduct and theology.

The Scriptures

One of the first things we teach new followers of Jesus is to read the word of God. We explain that this is an aspect of acknowledging Jesus as the Lord over our time. We begin the day with him. We allow him time to shape our characters and mould us into his ways. We take time to read and study his word. We make a daily commitment to spend time with the Lord we follow. In our life groups (as well as in Sunday school), we encourage new believers to memorize verses from the Bible. But whereas Muslims often memorize the Qur'an without understanding it, we make sure that people understand what they are memorizing.

Most Muslims know very little about the Scriptures, but the word of God, when read reflectively and prayerfully, has the power to transform. This is true even before someone becomes a believer. Abdul Saleeb, who is now a Christian follower of Jesus, has said he was struck by the contrast between the violent tone of many passages in the Qur'an and the emphasis on love in the New Testament. Thus one of the best gifts we can give to a Muslim friend is a copy of the New Testament. The word of God is alive and powerful and is able to restore lives (Heb 4:12; 1 Pet 1:23).

In our experience, Christians seldom offer a Bible to a Muslim. Some think that they might be offended or reject it; others think that there is no point in giving a Muslim a Bible since they believe the Bible has been corrupted. Too many assumptions are made about this. I have rarely encountered a Muslim who has refused to accept a Bible as a gift. Many Muslims have never read the Bible, just as many Christians, even missionaries to the Arab world, have never read the Qur'an. We all know about the holy book of the other, but have we actually read it ourselves? When we hand a Bible to a Muslim friend, we bring their lives close to the Word of life.

In some contexts, however, giving someone a Bible might cause them a lot of trouble. We should be sensitive to this possibility. But now that the Bible can be found online and can easily be accessed electronically, the risk of being assaulted by a spouse or a brother if caught in possession of a Bible is lessening.

In one of his tweets the late Nabeel Qureshi, a follower of Jesus from a Muslim background who was an active leader with a prominent organization, asserts: "I left Islam because I studied Muhammed's life. I accepted the gospel because I studied Jesus's life."

Another powerful testimony to the transforming power of the Bible is given by Sheikh Dr Mustafa Rashid, who is a scholar at Al-Azhar, president of the World Association of Islamic Scholars for Peace and Non-Violence, and president of the World Conscience Organization for Human Rights. He, too, has shared publicly about encountering Christ and the transformation he experienced. He tells that he became a sheikh in Al-Azhar because it was what his family wanted (many members of his family were sheikhs, including his grandfather).

> I was a Muslim. I learned Islam and taught it in Egypt and in other Arab countries. Once, a Christian brother asked me to attend the wedding of his nephew. So I thought I would enter the church to see what was happening in this place, and when I entered, I felt comfortable unlike what I expected. [Afterwards] I saw visions of a church and heard hymns in my dream. The dream was repeated three times. I saw myself standing at the door of the church, the hall was very long and at the end of the hall [was] a preacher and a ray of light. I could not see from the preacher anything except his piercing eyes, his hand that tells me to come near, and his smile. This was something very strange for me. I started to search for what was happening and went looking for a Bible. I went to the

church and asked for the gospel. A man who was at the church gave me a copy of the Sacred Book and some Christian books and offered to come to explain the word to me if I needed help in understanding it. After that I started reading in the book and it was difficult for me because I taught my students that if we held the Bible in our hands we would be defiled for forty days. [. . .] Then I began reading the twenty-seven books of the New Testament. Since I had memorized the Qur'an and the Hadith I was able to compare what the Qur'an says and what the Bible says. Of course, in the Qur'an, there are twenty-nine verses that give direct order for killing (fight the infidels, so strike [them] upon the necks and strike from them every fingertip) and 186 words talking about killing and its derivatives, but in the Gospels I found no verses of violence or blood, but on the contrary I saw it speak about supreme principles, and how God causes his sun to rise on the evil and the good and sends rain on the righteous and the unrighteous, and about blessing those who curse, and about loving your enemy. These are simple words and a beautiful way from violence and murder and hatred.[1]

I encourage those who are coming to the Bible for the first time to start with the Gospels. However, some of our leaders like to start with narratives from the book of Genesis (the Fall, the call of Abraham, Abraham's sacrifice of Isaac, etc.) and then move on to the Gospels. Still others suggest specific chapters from different books of the Bible until the seeker or new believer is ready to go through a whole book. No one pattern of Bible reading works for everyone.

The Nicene Creed

We also want new believers to understand that our church does not exist in isolation but is part of the wider church of God. So we need to be clear about exactly what the church believes. We set out to help new believers understand the faith by focusing on three key elements: the creed, baptism, and the Lord's Supper.

The creed we teach is the Nicene Creed, an ancient Spirit-led statement that sets out several core beliefs of the Christian faith. We have chosen to use this creed because it more comprehensive than the Apostles' Creed.

---

1. https://www.youtube.com/watch?v=hR07OkgBsJs (in Arabic).

We believe in one God, the Father almighty, maker of heaven and earth, of all things visible and invisible.

And in one Lord Jesus Christ, the only Son of God, begotten from the Father before all ages, God from God, Light from Light, true God from true God, begotten, not made; of the same essence as the Father. Through him all things were made.

For us and for our salvation he came down from heaven; he became incarnate by the Holy Spirit and the virgin Mary, and was made human. He was crucified for us under Pontius Pilate; he suffered and was buried. The third day he rose again, according to the Scriptures. He ascended to heaven and is seated at the right hand of the Father. He will come again with glory to judge the living and the dead. His kingdom will never end.

And we believe in the Holy Spirit, the Lord, the giver of life. He proceeds from the Father and the Son, and with the Father and the Son is worshiped and glorified. He spoke through the prophets.

We believe in one holy catholic and apostolic church. We affirm one baptism for the forgiveness of sins. We look forward to the resurrection of the dead, and to life in the world to come. Amen.[2]

This creed forms part of our pathway to discipleship course (see the Appendix). We teach it in life groups and to those getting baptized, always referring to specific verses from the Bible as the source of the creed. We sometimes recite it during our services.

Baptism

From the earliest times, baptism has been an integral part of Christianity. The resurrected Jesus commanded it when he told his followers to go "and make disciples of all the nations, baptizing them in the name of the Father and the Son and the Holy Spirit" (Matt 28:19). The fact that the three Persons are said to have a single "name" points to the fact that in publicly acknowledging our allegiance to Christ in baptism, we are also acknowledging our allegiance to the Father, Son and Holy Spirit. Baptism is also an acknowledgement that we belong to the community of faithful followers of Jesus.

---

2. Nicene Creed (translation © 1988, Faith Alive Christian Resources / Christian Reformed Church in North America). Used by permission. All rights reserved worldwide.

Jesus himself was baptized because, as he explained, "it is fitting for us to fulfil all righteousness" (Matt 3:15). In other words, he wanted to be baptized in order to show believers what God expects of his people. Note that he did not say "it is fitting for me" but "it is fitting for *us*," indicating that both John the Baptist (who did the baptizing) and Jesus (who received baptism) were doing what God wanted. John was preparing the way for Jesus by calling on people to confess and repent of their sins in preparation for the coming of God's kingdom (Matt 3:2). Jesus was baptized to show his solidarity with John's mission, identifying with all those who came for this new beginning with God, and when we are baptized, we show our solidarity with Christ. Paul puts it this way: "All of you who were baptized into Christ have clothed yourselves with Christ" (Gal 3:27 NASB). Baptism is a public testimony to our identification with Christ. It is a deed of transfer that says, "I am now the property of Jesus Christ. From now on, I belong to him and only him; I publicly follow him and only him."

Baptism is also a public proclamation that we believe that the historical Jesus did indeed die and rise from the dead. Paul makes this clear when he writes, "We were buried therefore with him by baptism into death, in order that, just as Christ was raised from the dead by the glory of the Father, we too might walk in newness of life" (Rom 6:4). Baptism thus symbolizes both the death and resurrection of Jesus. No other religion believes in both events. So those who choose to follow Jesus through baptism are publicly proclaiming that their source of spiritual and ethical authority comes entirely from the Bible and not from any other book or spiritual influence.

Finally, baptism is a public declaration that we are united with Christ in his death and resurrection. To the Colossians, Paul says, "having been buried with him in baptism, in which you were also raised with him through faith in the working of God, who raised him from the dead" (Col 2:12; see also Rom 6:5, 8). In baptism, we are buried "with him" and also raised up "with him." We are proclaiming our willingness to walk behind him in his death knowing that we will also share his resurrection. It is a lifelong and after-lifelong commitment to follow in his footsteps. It is a commitment to self-denial and victory.

In the Middle East, statements about identifying with Jesus in his suffering are far from merely theoretical. Someone from a non-Christian background who decides to get baptized will face a high level of persecution. Yet many still choose to get baptized in public.

We also take note of the fact that Paul uses the plural "you," not the singular, when talking about baptism. Although each person is baptized as an individual, there is great encouragement in being baptized as part of a sizeable group of new believers, as a communal act. This ensures that those who publicly and formally give their allegiance to Christ are automatically welcomed by a group of his followers and are perceived by outsiders not as scattered individuals but as part of a community.

There are times when we advise people to postpone baptism for their own safety. On other occasions, we may encourage someone to wait until their family members are ready to accept their baptism in order to protect them from ostracism. We do not want someone's newfound faith in Jesus to drive a wedge between them and their relatives; rather, it should move them to love and serve their families better. Because we want believers to feel that RCB is also their home, those who postpone baptism for the sake of their loved ones are welcome to share in the Lord's Supper and to lead different ministries.

The Lord's Supper/Holy Communion

Baptism is one of the earliest rituals in the church. The other is the Lord's Supper (which Christians also refer to as "Holy Communion" or "the Eucharist"). This ritual was instituted by Jesus the night before his crucifixion when he took a loaf of bread, gave thanks, broke it and gave it to his disturbed disciples, saying, "Take it; this is my body" (Mark 14:22). Then he took a cup and gave it to them to drink from, saying "This is my blood of the covenant, which is poured out for many" (Mark 14:24).

During the Lord's Supper, we come together as a church to give thanks (the original meaning of the word "Eucharist") to God for sending his Son to die for us on the cross and to remember what Christ has done for us. Participation in the Lord's Supper is a constant reminder that we are loved, forgiven, redeemed and restored and that the promises of God were fulfilled on the cross. It is a reminder that we are sons and daughters of the living God and that we anticipate sharing in his great banquet when he returns.

When we gather for the Lord's Supper, we have an opportunity to come closer to Christ with confidence and humility. We meet him by faith, confess our sins, declare our constant need for him and for his forgiveness, and allow our soul to embrace him and rest in his presence. We also openly express our unity as the one body of Christ. As Paul says, "we who are many are one body; for we all partake of the one bread" (1 Cor 10:17).

Paul also tells us to examine ourselves before God before we take communion, "For anyone who eats and drinks without discerning the body eats and drinks judgement on himself" (1 Cor 11:29). Some members of the church at Corinth had fallen into the sin of segregating and isolating themselves from others. Some of the richer members may not have waited for the poor before eating the Lord's Supper, or possibly Christians from a Jewish background did not mingle with those from a Gentile background because they did not feel comfortable with those who were different from themselves. But the Lord's Supper was meant to bring the body together. Paul wants believers to discern that they are parts of one body and not isolated individuals or subgroups.

Like baptism, partaking in the Lord's Supper is a public declaration of our new identity in Christ and our separation from the evil world. In 1 Corinthians 10:21, Paul says, "You cannot drink the cup of the Lord and the cup of demons. You cannot partake of the table of the Lord and the table of demons." When we join in the Lord's Supper, we profess our faith in Christ alone and show our gratitude for his salvation. We belong to him and to no other. We were bought with a high price, Paul says, and we cannot be enslaved to anyone else except God (Rom 6:22).

Finally, the Lord's Supper is an opportunity to proclaim Christ publicly, "For as often as you eat this bread and drink the cup, you proclaim the Lord's death until he comes" (1 Cor 11:26). It is a public declaration of what Jesus has done for us.

One cultural issue that has emerged in our church is that in an honor-and-shame culture which is immersed in hospitality, some first-time visitors take communion not because they are believers but because they fear intimidation or simply as an act of respect to their host. So we have tried various ways of ensuring that only followers of Jesus take communion. Having a separate gathering for communion after a Sunday morning service did not work because many refugees come in shared buses or taxis and need to return together. When we announced that communion was only open to those who had been baptized, some faithful followers of Jesus who were not able to be baptized because of persecution were somewhat offended and felt rejected. So now we have an open communion during our Sunday morning service, where we clearly explain what we are doing. Before breaking the bread, the person leading the service explains the importance and meaning of the Lord's Supper to the congregation. We also encourage life group leaders to follow up with their group members during the week in case more explanation or exhortation is needed.

We also often ask those who want to partake in communion to stand as a sign of their commitment to Christ. We find that this helps those distributing the bread and wine not to offer it to those who are not ready or to visitors who have come with family members for the first time.

Traditionally the church has celebrated Holy Communion using bread and wine, as Jesus did when he instituted this sacrament. However, in recent years, we have switched to using grape juice instead to be culturally sensitive to those from non-Christian backgrounds who have never used alcohol.

Conclusion

The Bible is our authority, but the creed, baptism, and the Lord's Supper discourage individuals from detaching themselves from the rich relational and spiritual experience that comes from belonging to the church community. When individuals feel rejected by their loved ones and start searching for a loving community, when families leave their homeland and travel for miles to seek safety, when people from various ethnic groups come together, when men and women with all their cultural baggage arrive on the doorstep of the church, the one thing that unites them all is the one God we worship in the Spirit, the one Christ we crown as Lord and Savior, the one Bible we read and memorize, the one creed we recite, the one baptism we experience, and the one supper we share. The act of worshiping and fellowshiping as one body is indispensable for the growth of each member of the body.

8

Growing

Those who follow Jesus and acknowledge him as their Lord want to be like him. This does not mean that we want to be exactly like him in every way, right down to growing a beard and wearing a tunic. What it does mean is that all Christians should want to be more like him in character, so that as we play our part in bringing about God's kingdom in this world, our lives will have a transformational impact. The way we can achieve this goal is by opening ourselves to the Spirit who makes us more and more like Christ as we live a Spirit-filled and Spirit-led life.

In this context it does not matter whether we believe that people receive the Spirit when they come to Christ (as is my own conviction) or whether we believe it happens later as a separate experience. What matters is that each of us experiences the power of the Holy Spirit in our life. We should never reject the Spirit Jesus promised to his church. He knew that we would need the Spirit's presence, and we dare not contradict him.

The Holy Spirit does many things for believers. As part of making us more like Jesus, he keeps us from sinning. In our own strength, we cannot but fail and fall. Temptation can be strong and persistent. Even a mature pastor can fall prey to various temptations in the church and on the Internet. The only way to deal with such temptations, and all temptations, is to keep our eyes on Jesus, making a daily commitment to a Spirit-filled, Spirit-led life.

The Fruit of the Spirit

The Holy Spirit's work is not just to stop us from doing things; it is also to do positive work within us. He is the one who grows the fruit of the Spirit in us, as the apostle Paul reminds us in Galatians 5:22–23. The evidence of that fruit in the lives of believers is one of the reasons many Muslims are choosing to follow Jesus, so let us pause to reflect on these fruit in the context of the Arab world.

Love

In Islam God is perceived, first and foremost, as "great." That is the meaning of the phrase *Allahu Akbar* – God is great. He is up there, far away, far greater than anything or anyone we could think of or imagine, and because he is so great, every devout Muslim needs to seek his mercy. God is the grand Master and we are his servants. Since the relationship of a Master and servant is contingent upon the Master's mercy, the servant has only one option: to please the Master through good deeds and continue to seek his mercy. God shows us mercy, but we cannot show God mercy in return. The relationship is always one way.

Christianity, however, is founded on the conviction that God is love. And since God is love, he is near and not far away. Because he loves us deeply, he has adopted us into his family and we have become his children. This relationship is contingent upon who God is and who we are, and not upon what we do or how we behave. Since love rather than mercy is the foundation, we enjoy a two-way relationship with God. God says, "I love you," and we in return say, "Dad, I love you, too." So Christianity and Islam differ at this foundational level.

The Islamic worldview affects the daily life of every Arab, even many secular Christian Arabs, whether they recognize it or not. For example, when I was growing up, my father used to say, "When I speak to you, do not look into my eyes; I am your dad." According to this worldview, children should look down in humility and seek their father's mercy. Citizens should keep their heads down and seek their leader's mercy. The law is ruthlessly enforced to frighten people into submission.

When I became a new creation in Christ, I embraced the Christ-centered worldview revealed in the Scriptures – and found that it changed my relationships as the fruit of love grew within me. Today, when my son misbehaves, I bend down to his level and say, "Son, look in my eyes. I love you, but this is not how you should behave." I no longer see leadership in terms of power but in terms of love and caring for others.

Note that I am not saying only that God loves, but that he *is* love. In giving us the gift of his Spirit, God gives us part of himself. Such love that gives freely, unconditionally and without seeking anything in return is a compelling witness to the world around us. It is drawing many Muslims to Christ. On countless occasions, Syrians, who occupied our land for many years, have asked us, "How come you love us so much? What kind of God do you worship?"

Joy

The world regards joy as synonymous with happiness – until they meet refugees who follow Jesus. Despite losing everything except their life, they continue to be filled with a joy that is rooted in their relationship with God and God's family. They have hope and joy in the midst of trials, persecution and displacement because their eyes are set on God their Protector. They are like Paul, who was in prison when he wrote to the Philippians, yet in his brief letter he refers fifteen times to "joy" or "rejoicing."

Since becoming part of the church, many refugees have experienced indescribable joy even though their financial or social situation remains unchanged. Many people have come forward and told us that the joy they see in people's faces and the joy they experience during the service are not found in their homes. "I came with deep sorrow and I leave with overflowing joy," one young man told me. Another mother said: "My kids have realized that I have become so joyful since I started coming to church." A man shared about his miserable past and how God had put a smile on his face since the day he gave his life to Jesus.

Peace

Is peace possible in the midst of war and conflict? It is. This peace that is the fruit of the Spirit is not the elimination of life's storms but tranquillity even though one is still being tossed about by them. An Iraqi woman once asked me to pray for her. Afterwards, she told me her story. She had lost her husband more than twenty years before. Then, just before she fled to Lebanon as a refugee, her only son died in a fire while he was alone at home. She had come to Lebanon with no husband, no children, and no home, yet I sensed how peaceful she was. It was as if her soul was resting in the arms of God, untouched by outward circumstances. I felt I should have asked her to pray for me and not vice versa.

The Greek word that is translated "peace" when speaking of the fruit of the Spirit is used to translate the Jewish concept of *shalom*, which is frequently referred to in the Old Testament. In Arabic, shalom is *salam*, a word that expresses the idea of completeness and wholeness. It is the kind of peace that was God's original intention for all of creation. It is not merely a personal experience but communal, even cosmic. It is the life of God in us, among us and around us. It is the breaking-in of the kingdom of God in our midst. It is the kind of peace that reflects the fullness of life that Jesus spoke of in John 10.

It is, as Paul describes it, the bringing together of heaven and earth in Christ. Those who walk in peace and make peace are the children of God. They reflect the character of our heavenly Father. They draw the world to God. With Paul, I can say that "the peace of God, which surpasses all understanding, will guard your hearts and your minds in Christ Jesus" (Phil 4:7).

Patience

Patience, longsuffering, forbearance, endurance of ill-treatment and persecution, and a conscious decision not to seek revenge are all included in the Greek compound word "long-tempered" that is translated as "patience." God is cultivating this fruit abundantly among many of those we work with – otherwise they would not be able to survive the things they are forced to endure. Take the mother forced to watch while her son was tortured and beheaded, knowing that if she closed her eyes, cried, or showed any emotion, her daughter would be killed too. This woman surely received an extra measure of patience to bear up and remain standing on that day, and on every day since then.

The same "long-temperedness" is commanded in Ephesians 4:2, where Paul says that those who believe in Christ must conduct themselves "with all humility and gentleness, with patience, bearing with one another in love." He uses the word again in Romans 12:19: "Beloved, never avenge yourselves, but leave it to the wrath of God, for it is written, 'Vengeance is mine, I will repay, says the Lord.'"

Kindness

Men often speak of how kind their wives have become after encountering Jesus. Their wives act with goodness and sweetness, and even when their faith and patience are tested, they respond with benevolence and kindness. One reason many non-Christian men do not forbid their wives from going to church is because of the kindness these women display at home and their adaptability in meeting their husbands' needs. Wives also speak of how friendly and kind their husbands become once they fully surrender their lives to Jesus. At her baptism, one woman testified that it was the kindness and friendliness of her husband after his conversion that drew her to accept Jesus too.

Goodness

The word "goodness" means to *be* good and to *do* well. Paul is referring to character, to moral excellence. It is about being good to everyone, regardless of their behavior. Goodness does not buy into the law of an eye for an eye and a tooth for a tooth. Those who have witnessed or endured bloodshed, corruption, injustice and retaliation can easily drift away from goodness, even if they are Christians. But being alive in Christ means swimming against the tide; dead fish float with the tide of worldly convention.

To be good is to imitate a good God, a God who is not pleased with bloodshed and who does not send his angels to choke people at night. He does not hurl down fire from heaven, nor does he incite hatred and killing. He is a good God – and always will be.

Instead of making God in our image, and thereby distorting who he is, we should allow him to operate through us in goodness and love so that we can display his image to this world. The Arab world is in dire need of such goodness.

Faithfulness

A faithful person is someone with great faith, who walks faithfully behind Christ. *Faithfulness* is trusting and following expressed in a single word. A faithful person is a man or woman of discipline, with an unwavering commitment to follow in the footsteps of their Master wherever that may lead them. Today, as in the early years of Christianity, many followers of Jesus are remaining faithful even to the point of martyrdom. In recent years, when the faith of Egyptian, Sudanese, Algerian and Syrian Christians was tested, many chose to die on the shore in their orange prison clothing rather than be unfaithful to their Lord. We saw their deaths on our TVs. Many others whom we do not know have endured torture and gone to be with the Lord rather than give up their faith and have their earthly lives spared.

Gentleness

Gentleness and meekness have seldom been considered virtues, but in Christ they have become so. Jesus was gentle and meek, though all-powerful and exalted. As a gentle person, he was able to rule his own spirit and his inner desires. When he corrected, people listened to him; when he pardoned, he did not brag about it; and when he showed kindness, people knew that his gentleness was the result of his strength and not a weakness. That is the sort of gentleness we need to show. Gentleness reflects a secure personality, a balanced character, a shepherding heart and a motherly soul. It is going the extra mile, turning the other cheek, and looking into the eyes of the enemy with meekness, yet without fear. It is winning when others think that we have lost. The Christian community is called to be gentle, especially with those who are different from us – refugees, strangers, and those who are ethnically unlike us. A gentle Christian does not throw stones, expel strangers, exploit the poor or fear the unjust.

Self-Control

The apostle Peter told the believers of his time to "make every effort to supplement your faith with virtue, and virtue with knowledge, and knowledge with self-control, and self-control with steadfastness, and steadfastness with godliness, and godliness with brotherly affection, and brotherly affection with love" (2 Pet 1:5–7). To have control over one's thoughts, over dark memories of the past and over one's behavior and actions is a fruit that is given by God to those who desperately need it, like the communities we work with. Those who have lost loved ones feel unable to control their anger and struggle with painful memories. Some become suicidal, others are filled with the desire to avenge their loss, still others lash out at God and at the people around them. Their reactions are understandable. They have suffered a great deal, experiencing first-hand what most of the world has only glimpsed on television screens from the safety of their homes.

Conclusion

The cultivation of the fruit of the Spirit, fully embraced and boldly lived out, is the key to the transformation of the Arab world. May the grace and power of God enable us – his disciples – to bear much fruit and bring glory to our Father in heaven.

9

Serving

When new believers are welcomed into our church, they are nurtured and encouraged to grow. We expect them to start manifesting evidence of the fruit of the Spirit in their lives, as we saw in the last chapter. But the Spirit does not only produce fruit; he also pours out special gifts for the edification of the church and the conversion of the world.

Many centuries ago, the prophet Joel, speaking on behalf of God, prophesied:

> And it shall come to pass afterward,
>> that I will pour out my Spirit on all flesh;
> your sons and your daughters shall prophesy,
>> your old men shall dream dreams,
> and your young men shall see visions. (Joel 2:28)

That prophecy was fulfilled on the day of Pentecost and continues to be realized in our midst by the power of the Holy Spirit, who lives in and among us. Stories of visions and dreams have already been mentioned in an earlier chapter. In this chapter, we will look at the many other spiritual gifts God gives to his children. Some of them are listed in Romans 12:6–8, 1 Corinthians 12:4–11, 28–30, Ephesians 4:7–12 and 1 Peter 4:10.

Using Spiritual Gifts

I will not attempt to list all the gifts or to classify them (using categories like gifts for practical service, gifts of power, gifts of utterance, and so on). Instead, what I will do here is show you how these gifts are at work in the growth and ministry of RCB, a church filled with refugees and followers of Jesus who come from non-Christian backgrounds. My goal is to challenge you to look for the gifts of the Spirit among those whom you seek to serve, and to nurture and encourage them wherever they are found. Discipleship grows as people use their gifts to serve the church.

Apostleship and evangelism

The Greek word "apostle" means "one who has been sent out." The gift of apostleship was initially given to the Twelve, but later it was also given to Paul, Barnabas, Andronicus, Junias (or Junia), and possibly to others like Silas and Timothy. An apostle's main ministry is to proclaim the good news to the unbelieving world, breaking new ground and reaching out to the community at large. Apostleship is thus closely associated with the gift of evangelism, that is, of preaching the gospel.

Believers with these gifts play a major role in the spread of the gospel. God is preparing many apostles among the refugees so that when they return to their home countries, whether Iraq or Syria, or even if they move to the West, they can proclaim Christ and start new churches.

At RCB, although we empathize with the painful struggle our beloved refugees go through, by faith we claim every refugee as a future apostle to whatever country they are sent. We have already seen many such apostles, both men and women, making disciples in Syria. We also have former refugees serving as missionaries in Australia, Turkey, Greece, Switzerland, Austria, Spain, Germany, France, Sweden, Denmark, the UK, the USA and Canada. These Syrian and Iraqi families are boldly sharing their faith in the new communities they find themselves in.

But these apostles face a number of challenges. First, there are spiritual challenges. In their new homes, they may not find a church in which they can grow spiritually. Second, the language barrier in Western countries hinders them from sharing Christ with the locals, and so they can only share Christ with refugees who speak similar languages. Third, many (though certainly not all) face rejection. In London, for example, a Lebanese Orthodox monk was assaulted because his appearance and long beard were interpreted as meaning that he was a radical Muslim. Our people are rejected just because they look different.

Our church seeks intentional partnerships with other churches to protect these unknown apostles and give them opportunities to grow. But even with such help, life is not easy. For example, one organization associated with a church helped Amal, a life group leader from a Kurdish background, to move to Argentina. She was promised a lot but received very little. Upon her arrival, she was driven to a rural area where she and her family were given a small house to stay in. Unfortunately, the organization did not think beyond this immediate need and did nothing to help her family integrate in the new community. She was lonely, she didn't know the language, she couldn't develop friendships, and the closest church was miles away from where she was staying. She called us and told us that she was in such turmoil that she had even been thinking of suicide. Eventually, she returned to Lebanon.

Although most Syrians are choosing to leave and go to the West because they cannot return to their villages, a few are hearing God's call to return to their homeland. Amina, from the city of Afrin in Syria, came to know Christ in Lebanon. She chose to go back to Syria and live and serve there. Her husband died recently, but her faith continues to sustain her, and her witness is powerful among her relatives and friends. Another Syrian family rejected the opportunity to leave Lebanon and chose instead to study theology at the Arab Baptist Theological Seminary in order to be better equipped to serve the Lord in Lebanon and Syria. These heroes are honored among us and should be supported to accomplish God's calling for their lives.

I believe that the children of those refugee apostles will play a pivotal role in bringing the gospel back to Europe and transforming the present culture of the Western world. It is only as you encounter the faith of these children and realize how the gospel has transformed their horrifying past that you can grasp their potential impact on Western society. The church in the Middle East is planting the seed of Christ in the hearts of these meek ones, who will one day inherit the earth and whose fruitfulness will bless many nations. These children understand the horrific impact of hatred and war. These children appreciate the moment and rejoice in the little they have. These children have learned to create toys out of the bones of cows and trash bags.

Are the world, and the church in particular, aware that these refugee children are going to become either the terrorists or the heroes of the future? Do we bear this in mind as we provide food vouchers, medication, milk, social clubs and activities, Bible stories and children's worship sessions? The future will make us all feel either proud or uncomfortable and remorseful that we did not invest enough love, care, education and spiritual guidance in all members of refugee families.

Prophecy

The gift of *prophecy* is powerfully manifested in our church, among both men and women. There have been instances where women have conveyed divine revelation and spoken God's truth to their husbands and children in times of need. On a regular basis, parents share how their children have spoken divine words that led them to stop an argument, to reconcile or to be brought closer to Christ. Words of edification, exhortation and consolation have kept many new followers of Jesus from reverting to their old way of living. There can be no doubt that the gift of prophecy has enriched the life of our church.

Teaching

In the list of gifts in Ephesians 4:11, the underlying Greek grammar makes it clear that the gifts of pastors and teachers are very closely connected. Their task is to preserve the tradition of Jesus and the early apostles, expound it, and interpret it in new contexts. Such teaching is essential for the growth of the church. In fact a major crisis faced by churches in the Middle East is the lack of solid biblical teaching and expository preaching.

At RCB, sound teaching has safeguarded our church from division. Visitors from the West sometimes ask how we manage to embrace refugees without losing our original church members. Sound teaching has enabled the congregation to understand how the "mystery" of Gentile inclusion that was revealed to Paul (Eph 3:6) speaks into our situation today. As Paul reminded the Ephesians, Jesus Christ has "made us both one and has broken down in his flesh the dividing wall of hostility . . . , that he might create in himself one new man in place of the two, so making peace, and might reconcile us both to God in one body through the cross, thereby killing the hostility" (Eph 2:14–17). Now that we as believers – whether from a Christian or Muslim background – "both have access in one Spirit to the Father," (Eph 2:18) how can we even consider refusing to embrace one another as one united body?

However, it is not enough for teachers or pastors just to know the Scriptures. If they wish to minister to an Arab congregation or to Arab refugees, they must also know something about the history of the Arab world and the present political, economic and social context. Then when they exercise the gift of teaching, in combination with the related gifts of the utterance of wisdom and knowledge (1 Cor 12:8), their message will be both biblically sound and contextually relevant to the needs of the congregation.

Such teaching will transform a whole congregation – longstanding members as much as newcomers. It helps us to contextualize the word of God so that it speaks with relevance and power into our daily situations. It helps us to develop principles that will speak to every generation. Good teaching makes a strong church.

Discernment

The gift of discernment or "distinguishing between spirits" (1 Cor 12:10) helps followers of Jesus discern whether utterances are true or false and distinguish between true and false prophets. Because there is a great deal of contradictory teaching in the Arab world, people need this gift to enable them to reject both the false teaching they have grown up with and false beliefs they come across after choosing to follow Jesus. The Arab world is being flooded with Christian teachings from the West. New Christians thirst for knowledge and are often eager to drink at any well, which means they desperately need God's gift of discernment.

Tongues and interpretation of tongues

Tongues and the interpretation of tongues are wonderful gifts that are intended mainly for personal edification. I do not doubt that they are still blessing those to whom they are given today. However, we seldom see much evidence of them in our work with refugees. To them, God manifests himself through visions and dreams, and they continue to experience the power of the Holy Spirit working in and through them in their daily lives.

Faith

Faith, as a gift given by the Spirit to individuals, is common among our brothers and sisters from non-Christian backgrounds, and is very necessary in the midst of trials and persecution. The exceptional faith that we see in their lives – enabling them to trust God for daily miracles – is a powerful witness to the presence of God in their midst. We often hear of miracles such as provision for daily physical needs, healing without going to a doctor, unexpected job opportunities, and being able to face persecution fearlessly. Or we are told that "our neighbor came and knocked on our door and gave us a stew the day we had no more food left," or "the church sent someone to give us bread (or milk) just when we had no more left." A parent will tell us, "my child was very sick and we had no money to take him to the doctor. I prayed for him and the next day he was fully recovered." Still others have shared how Christ gives them strength to hold on to their faith amid persecution, especially when it comes from family members.

Helping and mercy

The gifts of helping and mercy are also common at RCB, especially among refugees and displaced people. These powerless people who have suffered the tyranny of those in power are moved with compassion to serve others. They care for the sick and the needy in their community – those whom governments and militants have long neglected and abused. They even care for those who were once their enemies.

When the poor give generously to help other needy families, people notice. When a faithful follower of Jesus visits a refugee friend in hospital, or donates blood, or looks after children at home when the parents need to be elsewhere, or stands by parents who have lost their child in the war – all these acts of mercy reflect the love of Christ in a practical and powerful way. When people give their time, resources and energy, without hidden motives, they are fulfilling Paul's desire for the church to share with others cheerfully and generously (Rom 12:8).

Leadership and administration

God gives some people gifts of leadership and administration so that they can lead and direct local ministries of the church. The need for such gifts became very clear with the sudden influx of Syrians into Lebanon. Compassionate people were eager to respond, but we soon found that we needed capable administrators, managers and leaders to manage our growth, sustain our ministry and move us forward. We found that we lacked both human and material resources. We had volunteers, but they had limited time and other priorities and needed direction as to the best use of their time and how to carry their tasks out well. Moreover, the volunteers and the congregation came from a variety of backgrounds, making it easy for misunderstandings to arise. So God sent us people with gifts of leadership and administration to help steer the ship in the right direction with as few casualties as possible, and to help us carry out the vision and mission of the church.

Exhortation

The gift of exhortation is another important gift that we see being used in our faith community. Those with this gift comfort and encourage fellow believers and exhort new followers of Jesus to live out the teachings of Jesus that they are now encountering for the first time. They have a key role. For example, the pastor may preach a great sermon on "loving your neighbor" and someone may hear it, enjoy it, and then go home and beat his wife. It is the task of a gifted exhorter, working either with an individual or with a life group, to encourage deeper reflection on the teaching that has been given and to confront cultural norms. Only then will the sound biblical teaching start to affect how people live their everyday lives.

Similarly, a powerful teaching series on forgiveness may open past wounds, bringing back ugly images and painful memories of loved ones being tortured, raped, or killed. At such times, there is a great need for comforters and encouragers to stand by those who have been deeply hurt and to walk alongside them on the painful path of forgiveness.

Music and composing songs

In the midst of the refugees' pain, the Spirit speaks through gifted worshipers who compose songs in their native language that reflect the reality of life and their hope in God. Here is a translation of a song composed by one local musician:

> When desperation fills our hearts
> When the eyes of the lowly are filled with tears
> When war tears down our homes
> I cry out and say
>
> *Chorus*
> *You are the King of kings*
> *You are the Lord of Lords*
> *You are my affectionate Father*
> *You are strength and peace*
>
> When my day is filled with wounds
> And I journal about it with sorrow and tears
> When worries surround me
> I cry out and say
>
> *Chorus*
>
> When I do not know what lies ahead
> And where to go next
> When darkness is all around and there is no way out
> I cry out and say

Chorus

When wickedness cripples people
And their minds are hardened
When sin takes over
I cry out and say

Chorus

You are the joy,
You are the celebration
You will give us comfort soon
And we will meet for sure, oh Jesus

Chorus

In You our souls find life
And only goodness reigns
On earth and in every home
Jesus is the King of kings

Reading

Kurds and Arabs who never had any opportunity to go to school have shared how the Spirit is enabling them to learn to read and understand the Scriptures. Before, they may only have known something about the alphabet because they saw it on road signs, but now they are able to read whole sentences and paragraphs. They are delighting in their ability to read, something they have longed to be able to do since childhood. The Spirit is granting a love for his word, a passion to read, the perseverance to learn, and insight to understand.

Identifying Spiritual Gifts

There are many spiritual gifts, and each of us should work to discover what gifts God has blessed us with. We should encourage each other to examine our passions, experience, past, calling, personality, what people think of us, and areas in which we were successful in the past in order to discover our gifting and how God can use us in powerful ways in the future. The pathway to discipleship curriculum (see Appendix) includes a section dedicated to discovering our spiritual gifts. Women and children in particular are thrilled to discover how many gifts God has blessed them with and how much they can contribute to the body of Christ.

We should also beware of assuming that refugees only have needs and not gifts. They have much to give. We are not the only ones on whom God has bestowed spiritual and natural gifts. Through my relationship with refugees, I have discovered how gifted they are. Some are very practical, others have linguistic skills or teaching skills, others were doctors, lawyers, or engineers. Many believers among them have wonderful spiritual gifts and should be on church boards or teams, or leading ministries in the church themselves. We should train ourselves not to look at people in terms of their problems but in terms of their strengths and gifts.

Women are another group whose gifts are often not recognized. When I was invited to pastor Resurrection Church, women had no leadership positions. It was only when we empowered women to lead that our church grew in number, in the quality of discipleship, and in impact. We were forced to recognize that the most powerful yet untapped human resource in the Middle East and Northern Africa is women. Women are the first to receive visions and dreams, the first to come to faith in Jesus Christ, the first to mature in their faith, the first to lead the men in their families to Christ, and women are first to become life group leaders and lead different ministries.

Men are also indispensable, and the church will not continue to grow without the real involvement of faithful and godly men, husbands and fathers. In a patriarchal society, the need is always to empower women to use their gifts while doing so with great respect and honor to the men in the families. Men do not need to be promoted into leadership in the Arab world, nor do they need to be demoted so that women can lead. Rather, they need to learn how to continue to lead by following Jesus's example of servanthood and empowerment, without losing their gift of protecting and providing for the needs of their family.

In every aspect of our life and work, all of us must seek to be Spirit-led, accountable to the invisible Christ, who is present with us. Our goal must always be to make Christ visible to those around us through our character, rich in the fruit of the Spirit, and the work we do with the gifts he has given us.

10

Freeing and Healing

We may be discipling refugees, teaching them, walking with them, encouraging the fruit of the Spirit in their lives and the use of their gifts in the church, but sometimes all that is not enough. Sometimes they also need freeing and healing.

This was brought home to me again in March 2017 when I was in Oslo, Norway, speaking at a conference and in a few churches. I was introduced to a family from a Christian background from Syria. The man's name was Sameer. Every Sunday, Sameer and his family watch our church service live on SAT7.

Sameer shared his story with me. In 2013 he was stopped at the border between Lebanon and Syria by the Free Army. They ordered him off the bus, put a gun to his head and made him kneel on the ground. Then they asked his religion. In his heart, he heard Christ's voice telling him, "Whoever denies me before men, I also will deny before my Father who is in heaven" (Matt 10:33). So he said to himself, "Since I am going to die, let me die as a Christian." Terrified, he said, "I am a Christian." To his amazement, the man who had asked the question looked up towards heaven and then ordered him to get back on the bus.

Sameer now lives in Oslo with his wife and two little boys, and his wife is pregnant with their third child. But it was clear to me as I was listening to him that this man is still bound by what happened to him. He needs deep healing and freedom from the past and the hatred he now has towards Muslims. Others who have suffered unimaginable horrors share a similar need.

Of course, not every refugee is traumatized to this extent. Some families managed to flee with few casualties; many felt protected and did not experience death or physical pain. Most did lose their homes and possessions but are thankful that their lives were spared. Many of those who have come to Christ even feel thankful to God for the turmoil, which led them out of spiritual death and into life with Jesus. Yet, broadly speaking, everyone has suffered, but to varying degrees.

Who can set these people free from their emotional pain? Who can bring healing to their souls? Who can rebuke the evil one who has found his way into their lives, and capture their past, memories, feelings, mind and future? The best institution on earth to really help these broken-hearted people is the church, the body of Christ who "went about doing good and healing all who were oppressed by the devil" (Acts 10:38).

Throughout his ministry, Jesus cast out demons and freed people from bondage. In Luke 11:20, Jesus explained to his adversaries that casting out demons is one clear evidence of the arrival of the kingdom of God: "If I cast out demons by the finger of God, then the kingdom of God has come upon you." Moreover, through his cross, resurrection and ascension, Jesus triumphed over rulers and authorities, disarming them and making a public display of them (Col 2:15), and ever since, all angels, authorities and powers are subjected to him (1 Pet 3:22).

Jesus's power to cast out demons, as well as his death and resurrection, perfectly demonstrate the power of God over the evil spirits, the destruction of Satan's kingdom, the restoration of human freedom and the reign of God over all. And the role of Christ's church is to bring individuals under the lordship of Christ in the kingdom of God. When we proclaim Christ, demons flee and God reigns. Casting out demons and proclaiming God's reign are two sides of the same coin.

Freeing

I have vivid memories of an incident that happened among us just a few months before we started to work with refugees. I was preaching at one of our church conferences. In the first pew was a woman from a non-Christian background who was visiting our church for the first time. As I was preaching, she became more and more agitated and started to scream whenever she heard the name of Jesus. A woman leader from our church, who happened to be sitting next to her, put her hand on her and started to pray for her. The demon in her resisted coming out and caused her to become even more distressed. More leaders and believers came and laid hands on her (or on others who had their hands on her) and kept praying, until almost the whole church was laying hands on each other and praying for the demon to come out. All of a sudden she screamed and fell to the ground silently. The demon had left her. Afterwards, I learned that the previous night about ten people in our church had had evil dreams and been left disturbed by what they saw.

Incidents like that have helped us at RCB to realize that freeing people from bondage needs to be integrated in the various ministries of the church. We have also come to recognize that Jesus differentiated between physical healing and exorcism. For example, he gave his disciples "authority over unclean spirits, to cast them out, and to heal every disease and every affliction" (Matt 10:1). The disciples used this authority to do these two things, for in Mark 6:13 we read that they drove out demons and also anointed many who were sick and healed them. So we have good grounds for making this distinction.

As someone with a Baptist background and a PhD in theology from Birmingham University, I am not accustomed to casting out demons; it is maybe the last thing I consider doing when I meet people in bondage. So do not assume that when I talk about freeing I am automatically referring to exorcism. But the bottom line here is that Jesus freed people from bondage, and we ought to be faithful and follow in his footsteps.

Many of those who come to us appear to be well physically, but they are broken emotionally, mentally and relationally. They are trapped in a painful past, with bad memories that constantly trouble them, or they live in fear and unrelenting anxiety. Some have witnessed the death of loved ones; others have been abused sexually, verbally or physically; still others have been tortured and have had to flee their homes with little or no assistance. They come to us hurting and broken and they seek freedom from something within and around them that is continuously suffocating and attacking them.

It is sometimes hard to differentiate between psychological problems like this and demon possession, but regardless of the source of the problem, God wants to restore human freedom. He can use the gift of exorcism, the skills of a psychologist, the experience of a counsellor or the intuition of a pastor to set people free.

Here are some practical ways in which the church can stand by suffering people and set about freeing them:

- Initiate life groups (or home groups or small groups) in their homes. Life Groups are the number one tool to bring healing to families. When we invite ourselves to their homes, they feel appreciated and loved. Suddenly, they become the host and we become their guests. In life groups, we listen, we love one another, we share our lives together, we read the Word, we pray for freedom and healing. Life groups are necessary should we want to see healing take place among us.

- Encourage life groups to use what we call "freedom classes" to explore holistic healing. The materials we have developed for these classes cover subjects like healing after trauma, understanding suffering, healing wounds, what happens when someone is grieving, taking our pain to the cross, and how we can forgive others. These classes can be powerful tools, especially when the group leaders are competent and capable of addressing deep issues within their group. Many people have spoken of the healing that takes place during these sessions.
- Allow space for prayer after the Word is preached each Sunday. In our church, we have extended the time of the church services to accommodate more prayer after the service. There is almost always an invitation for people to come and give their lives to Jesus, to crown him as Lord over their lives, and an invitation to come for prayer to experience healing and freedom.
- Develop trauma counselling teams to serve people with specific needs. At our church, we have more than ten counsellors who are able to assist and help with difficult cases. These counsellors should be trained professionals as well as people of prayer and discernment.

Casting out evil spirits on a one-to-one basis, inviting professionals to dig deep in someone's past, or having experts deal with the present and bring transformation are all good and helpful approaches to freeing people from bondage. Many churchgoers would prefer the pastor to pray over them, but wise pastors make sure to introduce other leaders at an early stage and involve them in the counselling ministry, as well as communicating to the congregation the importance of seeking help from their life group leaders (especially when the need is so great).

Healing

In Psalm 103:1–3, David proclaims God's goodness by saying:

> Bless the LORD, O my soul,
>> and all that is within me,
>> bless his holy name!
> Bless the LORD, O my soul,
>> and forget not all his benefits,
> who forgives all your iniquity,
>> who heals all your diseases.

Disease, ill-health and physical needs are varied and widespread, especially for those who are displaced, broken, poor, miserable and homeless. How does the church respond to such need?

In the Bible, Christ paid attention to people's bodies and constantly healed physical ailments (Matt 4:23–25). He did not see the body as evil but as created by God, and in his kingdom, and so as something that should be restored. Jesus's bodily resurrection is further powerful evidence that the physical body matters to God. In eternity, the perishable will put on the imperishable, and the mortal will be clothed with immortality (1 Cor 15:54). We will not be raised into eternity without spiritual bodies of some kind.

Jesus also sent his disciples out to heal and to perform mighty deeds (Matt 10:8). It is thus clear that the physical dimension of human life should never be neglected, and the church is to use all possible means to bring physical healing. At RCB, we have seen God at work healing people. While we have not experienced dead people being raised to life or healings from paralysis or blindness, we have heard many testimonies to healing that has come in many forms, for God works in many ways. Here are some of those testimonies, roughly categorized in terms of the ways in which God was at work.

Divine intervention to prevent physical harm

Sometimes God heals by acting to prevent harm that might otherwise have befallen people.

- Individuals have shared how shells fell near them yet did not explode, or of burning houses from which those inside were saved in an extraordinary way.
- Families and individuals were stopped at checkpoints by radical groups, and while others on the same bus were killed, they were miraculously freed after some unexpected incident.
- Individuals felt they should take a different route or leave their home earlier than usual and so escaped certain death or car bombings.
- Jailed and tortured individuals who were expecting death cried out to God and were freed without knowing why.
- Individuals were released from captivity straight after people prayed for them in small groups.
- Individuals received calls from missing loved ones straight after they were prayed for, whether in small groups or privately.

- Families felt they must leave their city or village, and soon after doing so learned that ISIS had arrived and subjugated everyone who had remained behind.
- Teenage girls who were being pressured to marry ISIS soldiers or leaders were inexplicably able to flee at night with their mothers.
- Individuals kidnapped for ransom were released for unknown reasons through prayer.
- During construction work on our church, a partially blind individual fell down an empty elevator shaft from the fourth floor. He missed dozens of iron bars sticking out into the shaft and landed safely in a container of water about half a metre deep, without suffering even a scratch.

Direct divine healing

Sometimes God heals directly by restoring the physical body or alleviating a mental or emotional state.

- Many women have become pregnant after church leaders, male and female, prayed for them.
- A boy with cancer was prayed for one Sunday morning, and the following week tests showed that the cancer had completely gone from his body.
- Some of our leaders have witnessed healing from diabetes, thyroid dysfunction, swelling of legs and arms, severe back pain, eye problems, abdominal pain and severe/constant headaches. (It should be noted that these types of healing are rare.)
- A number of families who had no access to a doctor or a hospital have shared how they were healed from fevers, infection, bleeding or physical pain.

Indirect divine healing

Sometimes God heals indirectly through medical personnel and the medical knowledge he has given us access to.

- Many have seen their health improve and have been healed from disease or pain because the church was able to help them with medication or paid for a consultation with a doctor.

- Many cases of healing from hunger have occurred because God moved the hearts of believers (and unbelievers) to specifically serve someone who had been desperately calling to God for help. The type of help that was given included getting milk for children, bringing bags of food and loaves of bread, paying a family's rent, or giving someone money to start a small business selling goods.

Prevention of illness

God is also indirectly at work when we work to protect people from illness, and we believe this is another form of healing. Here are some of the things we teach and encourage people to do:

- Have regular check-ups.
- Eat healthily. The food packages the church provides for refugees contain healthy food, not junk food.
- Exercise. Many refugees do not have jobs and so spend most of the day sitting in front of the TV or sleeping. It is good for them mentally and physically if they get some exercise.
- Practise good general hygiene.
- Wear a seatbelt in the car.
- Respond biblically to illnesses. Some Christians from outside Lebanon have prayed and proclaimed healing over people and told them not to go to doctors because they are healed by faith. We do the opposite. We pray for people and tell them explicitly to go to their doctors and to follow their doctor's advice.

Conclusion

Although freeing and healing are not at the heart of our ministry, they are an important part of our witness. If we neglect the cry of the hurting, they will reject the message we are offering. Would a mother accept the message of Jesus when the messenger neglects the pain of her starving child? Caring for a person holistically brings restoration to the soul.

11

Praying

In the previous chapters we have often referred to the importance of praying with and for people, and you may feel surprised that I dedicate a whole chapter to the topic of prayer. There are three reasons for this. The first is that regular prayer is one of the five pillars of Islam. For many of our Muslim-background believers, prayer has been a central element in their lives. But there is a difference between Christian prayer and Muslim prayer, and this is something we need to recognize and help them to recognize. The second reason is that if we want to disciple believers so that they follow in the footsteps of Jesus, we should encourage them to live a life of prayer as he did. The third reason why I strongly recommend bringing prayer back to the heart of our teaching and ministries is that it has proven to be a powerful tool of transformation in our ministry among Muslims. We can pray for them and for their loved ones, we can also teach them how to pray and connect to God.[1]

Prayer in the New Testament

One of the earliest accounts of Jesus presents him as a man of prayer. Mark tells us right at the beginning of his gospel that "in the early morning, while it was still dark, Jesus got up, left the house, and went away to a secluded place, and was praying there" (Mark 1:35 NASB).

Although in Mark we see Jesus praying only two other times (Mark 6:46 – after the feeding of the five thousand; Mark 14:32–42 – in Gethsemane), both were at critical times. On both occasions he was praying at night and in solitude (as he did in the wilderness when he confronted the devil) and on both occasions he was praying because he needed to be strengthened by God the Father.

---

1. Arab scholars have in the past seen an etymological relationship between the word "prayer" (*salat*) and the word "connection" (*silat*).

Luke's gospel tells us much more about the prayer life of Jesus. He prayed during his baptism (Luke 3:21); he prayed when the news about him spread and many came to hear him and be healed (Luke 5:16); he spent the night in prayer just before he chose his twelve disciples (Luke 6:12); Peter's confession that Jesus was the Messiah took place in the context of prayer (Luke 9:18); the transfiguration occurred while Jesus was praying (Luke 9:28–29). We also learn that the disciples asked him to teach them how to pray (Luke 11:1) and that he instructed them to "stay awake at all times, praying that you may have strength to escape all these things that are about to take place, and to stand before the Son of Man" (Luke 21:36). Later we see Jesus praying for Peter before his denial (Luke 22:31–32); praying for the forgiveness of all on the cross (Luke 23:34), and finally, as he breathed his last, praying, "Father into your hands I commit my spirit" (Luke 23:46).

What did Jesus pray for? In Mark 14:35, Matthew 26:39 and Luke 22:41, he prayed for himself. In Luke 22:32, he interceded for Peter. In John 17:6–19, he prayed for his disciples and for their unity, and in John 17:20–26, he prayed for the whole church. In Luke 23:34, he prayed for those who nailed him to the cross. Sometimes our prayers can be inward-looking, focusing on ourselves and on our own needs. Jesus's example reminds us to pray looking outwards, praying not just for our family and friends, but for our church and its leaders, our community, our country, our government, the world – and even for our enemies.

Jesus frequently taught on the topic of prayer. In Matthew 6:5–8, he teaches against meaningless repetitive prayers "offered under the misconception that mere length will make prayers efficacious."[2] He detested the mechanical repetition of a specific formula without thoughtfulness and meditation. He also objected to those who offer lengthy prayers "for show" (Mark 12:40; Luke 20:47). In contrast to meaningless prayers, Jesus offers a model of how we should pray in Matthew 6:9–13, followed by a commentary that is connected with reciprocal forgiveness – "For if you forgive others their trespasses, your heavenly Father will also forgive you, but if you do not forgive others their trespasses, neither will your Father forgive your trespasses" (Matt 6:14–15, see also Mark 11:25).

Jesus taught that faith and watchfulness are important ingredients in the prayer life of his disciples (on faith, see Mark 11:24; Matt 21:22; on watchfulness, see Mark 13:33; Mark 14:38; Luke 26:41). In prayer, the disciples receive the

---

2. D. A. Carson, *Matthew,* Expositor's Bible Commentary, vol. 8 (Grand Rapids: Zondervan, 1984), 166.

Holy Spirit (Luke 11:13; see also Luke 24:49; Acts 1:8, 14; 2:1–4) and ask the Lord to send "laborers into his harvest" (Matt 9:38; Luke 10:2). In prayer, we may be delivered from temptation (Matt 6:13; 26:41; Mark 14:38; Luke 11:4; 22:40, 46). In prayer, we request our daily food (Matt 6:11 and Luke 11:3) and ask for deliverance from calamities (Mark 13:18 and Matt 24:20). In prayer, the breaking-in of the kingdom of God takes place in our world and people are freed from the dominion of Satan (Matt 6:10; Luke 11:2; Matt 17:21; Mark 9:29).

There are three parables in the Gospels that address the topic of prayer directly, and one that does so indirectly (two if you take the words of the Prodigal Son in Luke 15:18–19, 21 as a penitential prayer). The parable of the friend at midnight (Luke 11:5–8) teaches the importance of persistent prayer. So does the parable of the unjust judge (Luke 18:1–8). The parable of the tax collector and the Pharisee (Luke 18:10–14) teaches the importance of humility and on having an attitude of unworthiness when we approach God in prayer. The parable of the unjust servant (Matt 18:21–35) insists on charity and forgiveness. Because our Lord is compassionate and merciful, we are to show the same qualities. Those who are forgiven must forgive, and God answers the prayer of a forgiving heart.

In the book of Acts and the Epistles, prayer plays a vital part in the life of the early church. The church was born in the context of prayer and the Spirit fell on the church in an atmosphere of prayer (Acts 1:4, 14; 2:1–4). Later on, we see that prayer became an integral part of the life of the church: "we will devote ourselves to prayer" (Acts 6:4); "but earnest prayer for him was made to God by the church" (Acts 12:5); "About midnight Paul and Silas were praying and singing hymns to God" (Acts 16:25); "kneeling [. . .] we prayed" (Acts 21:5); "and prayed, and putting his hands on him" (Acts 28:8) (see also Acts 2:42; 4:23– 31; 6:6; 9:40; 10:9; 12:12; 20:36). The first thing we know about Paul after his conversion is that he was praying (Acts 9:11). Paul recorded over forty prayers in his letters, including instructions to pray (Rom 1:8–10; 10:1; 12:12; 15:5–6, 13; 15:30–33).[3] This certainly suggests that Paul, like his Lord, used to set aside specific times to pray for his fellow believers.

The writer of the Epistle to the Hebrews focuses on the role of Jesus as our High Priest, reminding us that because of him, we can draw near to the throne of grace (or in other words, pray) with confidence (Heb 4:14–16). James has three important passages on prayer. The first focuses on encouraging his

---

3. For a comprehensive list, see: http://www.kevinhalloran.net/the-apostle-pauls-prayers-in-the-bible/.

readers to pray and confidently ask God for wisdom because God is generous and gives abundantly (Jas 1:5–8). The second is in 4:1–3, where James addresses wrong motives for prayer. Third, James encourages his readers to pray in times of sickness (5:13–18). In his first letter, John has two explicit references to prayer, in 3:21–22 and 5:13–18. In both instances, there is a strong emphasis that God hears us whatever we ask. Moreover, he answers our requests if we live in obedience (3:22) and when our requests are asked according to his will (5:14).

It is thus clear that Jesus provided a powerful prayer model for the church, and that the early church was grounded in a close and intimate relationship with the Father through prayer.

Christian Prayer and Muslim Prayer

Some of the principles about prayer that we learn from the New Testament are important to highlight in the context of our ministry among Muslims.

The nature of prayer

The prayerful life of Jesus and his disciples was not a religious obligation but a practice woven into their daily life. Prayer is communing with God and seeking his will in all life circumstances. There are plenty of stories of transformation based on powerful encounters with God through prayer and of Muslims experiencing the presence of God in a mighty way while praying.

When to pray

There is no set time for prayer in the teaching of Jesus. The Islamic tradition based on the teaching of the Qur'an and the Hadith (a collection of the teachings, words and deeds of Muhammad) refers to several kinds of prayer. One of these is obligatory and consists of set prayers performed five times a day. There is a designated time for these prayers: early morning, dawn, midday, mid-afternoon and sunset. There is nothing equivalent in Christianity. Although some church traditions do have set hours for prayer, they readily admit that those hours are neither prescribed in the Bible nor mandatory for all believers.

Where to pray

In the New Testament, we read of prayers being offered in the temple in Jerusalem (Acts 3:1) and all kinds of other places, including outdoors (Acts 21:5), in homes (Matt 6:6; Acts 2:42, 46b), and in prisons (Acts 16:25). When Jesus said, "Behold, I am with you always, to the end of the age" (Matt 28:20), the disciples believed him and prayed accordingly. Men, women and children were happy to kneel in public on a beach and pray for the safety and protection of their friends and leaders (Acts 21:5). Today, however, Christians are often hesitant to pray in public places. We need to remember that Muslims have no problem with praying in the open air. Their boldness in doing so invites us to be more confident in praying in public places.

What to do before praying

Islam stresses the importance of physical purity before each session of prayer. Those who pray must first ritually cleanse their hands, nose, face, forearms, ears and feet. However, Jesus taught that the type of purity that is important to God is purity of heart. He does not require physical purity or any ritual cleansing before we can pray. What he does want to see is an attitude of faith, humility, simplicity of heart, charity and forgiveness. Similar attitudes are also required in Islam: Borrowing from the teaching of Jesus in Matthew 6:5–8, the Qur'an condemns those who "are unmindful of their prayer, or who pray only to be seen by people" (Qur'an 107:4–6).

Posture when praying

The Bible does not emphasize any particular physical posture when praying. People can pray kneeling, standing or lifting up their hands. Muslim worshipers are obliged to perform a cycle of four postures during the five daily prayers – standing, bowing, prostrating and sitting. The Christians' freedom of posture is well received when it is taught with reverence to God. It allows individuals to pray freely yet respectfully.

To whom we pray

All Arabic speakers, whether Christian or Muslim, pray to Allah, for *Allah* is the standard Arabic word for God that was in use among the Arabs a long time before the appearance of Islam (it actually comes from the Syriac/Aramaic language). What is distinctive in Christian prayer is that the prayer is generally offered to God the Father (Acts 4:24; 2 Cor 1:3) in the name of Jesus Christ (Rom 1:8). Christians also pray to Jesus Christ (Acts 1:24; 7:59; 1 Tim 1:12).

The content of our prayers

Some aspects of Christian and Muslim prayer are similar. In prayer, both Christians and Muslims acknowledge their weaknesses and their need for God's mercy and forgiveness. They also both praise God. For example, during their five daily prayers, Muslims recite phrases such as "Allah is greater," "Praise be to my mighty Lord," and "Allah hears the one who praises him." Similar praise is common in the Jewish holy book that we know as the Old Testament, and is also found in the Qur'an. It is also found in the Gospels and in the Epistles in the New Testament. But it is striking that in the New Testament there is far more thanksgiving than praise. (For the Gospels see Matt 11:25–26; 26:27; Luke 10:21; John 6:11; 11:41, and for the Epistles see Col 1:3; 1 Thess 1:2–3; 2:13–16; 3:9; 2 Thess 1:3; 2 Tim 1:3–7; Phlm 4–7.)

There is also one marked difference in content between Christian and Muslim prayers. In their set prayers, Muslims recite the first chapter of the Qur'an or other verses from the Qur'an, the Shahada (confession of faith), and the greeting of peace to all Muslims. But the idea of praying for and even blessing one's enemies is utterly foreign to Muslims, and is almost always received with amazement and awe. Muslims pray for victory over their enemies (Sura 3:147). Yet Jesus taught us to pray for and on behalf of everyone, including our enemies (Matt 5:44; 1 Tim 2:1) and there is strong biblical evidence for Christians praying such prayers. Stephen, the first Christian martyr, who seems to have had a great influence on Saul of Tarsus, followed his Master in forgiving and blessing his enemies (Acts 7:60). Saul, who later became Paul, taught the church in Rome to "bless those who persecute you" (Rom 12:14).

What to expect when we pray

In the New Testament, there are high expectations that God hears and answers prayers (Matt 7:7–8; 1 John 3:21–22; 5:13–18). There are also narratives that demonstrate God's intervention for his people (Acts 4:31; 16:25–26). Our Muslim neighbors need to hear these stories that stir faith and encourage them to seek God more in their daily lives. Many of our Muslim friends tell us that what God wants will always take place despite their prayers and requests. Yet others tell us that when we pray for them, God answers our prayers. Still others share with us that since they have come to Christ, they feel God answers their prayers regularly.

Praying the Lord's Prayer

There is much we and Muslim-background believers can learn from the prayer that Jesus taught to his disciples (Matt 6:9–13). Its content surely reflects Jesus's own theological beliefs and convictions about how we should pray and what we should ask for.

Our Father

No Muslim would refer to God as Father. Addressing him in this way is a powerful reminder that we have a much deeper and more intimate way of connecting to God. To call him "our Father" is to signal that we are in a relationship with him, a relationship based on his perfect love and grace. Our Father is near. He listens.

The "our" in the Our Father is also a communal sign, a confession that we are together, a community, as sons and daughters of the living God. It also reveals that we are not the children of this world but are the free children of God. It carries a promise that we are not in slavery and bondage. We are the children of the God who keeps his promises.

"Our Father" is an identity badge, a shining light in the darkness, a commitment that we, his children, will reflect the image of our Dad. It is also a child's call for help, a call that reflects our full dependency on our Dad, without whom we can do nothing in this world.

Who art in heaven

When we remind ourselves that the one whom we address as "Our Father" is in heaven, we adopt the right attitude towards God. We come into an intimate relationship, but we come in with reverence and holy fear because our Father is the Almighty God who rules over all.

In some parts of the Western world, we have taken "our Father" and dropped "who art in heaven," and in parts of the Arab world we have dropped "our Father" and kept "who art in heaven." Christ came to reveal both truths. I believe that the Arab world, which rightly respects God as "the greatest," is desperately in need of learning to know him as "our Father" as revealed in Christ.

Hallowed be thy name

In ancient times, and still today in the Arab world, names are closely connected with the person who carries the name. So most Arabic names have meanings that anticipate that this baby will one day become the meaning of their name.

In Arab culture, it is also utterly unacceptable to profane the name of your father. Instead, his name should be honored and preserved by subsequent generations. When Jesus said in the context of prayer, "Hallowed be thy name," he probably meant that God, who is holy, should be honored and treated as holy by us and all his creation.

Thy kingdom come

When we pray "Thy kingdom come" some Christians assume that they are praying for Jesus to return and take us to be with himself. But that interpretation is far too shallow. We are not simply asking to go to be with Jesus, we are also asking for his rule to come over us in the midst of our daily life. Through prayer we seek his divine dominion in this present age. This is what we want when we acknowledge Jesus as King.

Thy will be done on earth as it is in heaven

How powerful this prayer is, and how greatly it is needed in the midst of the injustice, death, displacement and hunger that we see in the Middle East. The uninterrupted prayer of the church in the midst of all the atrocities is this: "Lord, may you fully accomplish your will on earth as it is in heaven. When shells fall from the sky, when our children are kidnapped, when we hear that our loved ones have been raped and killed, when we lose everything, we turn to you with hope that you can transform these evil realities and we cry out for your will to 'be done on earth as it is in heaven.'"

Like the previous two petitions, this petition is totally centered on God. We pray in full commitment to hallow God's name, submit to his sovereignty and to do his will.

Give us this day our daily bread

In the Arab world, "our daily bread" represents the basic necessities of life. We know that when people are enduring severe hardship, they ask for simple things. In the morning, they ask for bread for the day, and in the evening, they ask for bread for the next day. It is hard to express how I felt on one occasion when I was approached by a refugee widow asking me to pray that God would provide for her basic needs. She had lost her husband and her only son in the Iraqi war, as well as her possessions and her home. Yet on that same Sunday, another person, who had almost everything they needed, was complaining about nonsensical things and praying a prayer that was filled with selfishness and materialism.

"Give us our daily bread" is the paradoxical cry of the meek who will one day inherit the earth.

And forgive us our debts, as we also have forgiven our debtors

In a world of turmoil, insecurity, war, displacement and loss, "forgive us our debts" is a confession that we ourselves are guilty and have also sinned. When people lose their loved ones, become displaced and wander with their little ones from one place to another, not only do they look in the eyes of the living and feel guilty for those who have died ("Could I have done something?"), they also feel indebted to those who are helping them.

"Pastor," said one Syrian who had had a leading position in his community, "what you see today in the Arab world is all because of us and because of our forefathers. Since we were born, we have been listening to stories of hate and killing. Brothers detest one another, leaders continuously stab one another in the back, governments hate their own people, riots and disturbances are everywhere. We have sinned and we are guilty for turning the Arab world into a living hell." I wish Western countries that have had a continuous interest in the Arab world since the fall of the Ottoman Empire would make a similar confession.

The second part of the prayer is also of great relevance: "as we also have forgiven our debtors." I would not be exaggerating if I said that almost all the refugees who have entered our church have been full of hatred and thirsty for revenge. Including the women and children. In our pre-school, one Syrian child was almost two years old when he uttered his first word (which becomes three when translated into English): "I hate you."

Another Syrian child fled with his parents and brother from Syria where they had seen many atrocities. At the age of three, as he was playing with his younger brother, he picked up a knife and started cutting his brother's throat. His parents heard the yelling and rushed their child to the hospital. When one of our church leaders asked him why he had attacked his brother, he said, "I was playing with him."

How do women feel when they have seen their children raped in front of their eyes? How do men feel when their closest family members are stoned or pushed off a cliff or shot dead for some unknown reason? This is why there is so much hatred in the Arab world.

Now, in the new kingdom, anyone who wishes to enter its gate of grace and forgiveness must also extend forgiveness to others in the community. Countless times people have told us that after they had given their hearts to Jesus, they experienced not only the forgiveness of their sins but also an immeasurable amount of love for their enemies and a humanly unexplainable attitude of forgiveness towards others.

And lead us not into temptation but deliver us from evil

For those who lived in earlier centuries, and still today in the Arab world, life is unpredictable, testing is inevitable, and persecution can come at any time. This final petition in the Lord's Prayer is a cry for protection and deliverance. It is a statement that says that everyone, including our rulers, have failed us so that we barely survive in an era of brokenness and misery, with the unavoidable tribulation looming on the horizons as a result of our present deeds. So we turn to God to give us endurance in the trials, and we ask him to deliver us from the evil sphere of life that has become the toxic oxygen we breathe day and night.

For Thine is the kingdom, and the power, and the glory, forever. Amen

Although the earliest and most authoritative manuscripts do not have this doxology, it has been used in the Christian church from an early time. It brings hope to a hopeless world and beautifully concludes the prayer that teaches *how* to pray and not *what* to pray. This prayer is a wonderful paradigm and a great model to replicate with great flexibility (compare Matt 6:9–13 with Luke 11:2–4) while maintaining the spirit of this prayer taught by our Lord.

Conclusion

Jesus communed with the Father (John 11:41–42; 12:28) and the church follows in his footsteps. Through the work of the Holy Spirit and in the name of Jesus, the church has full access to a caring heavenly Father whom Jesus revealed. This intimate relationship in prayer is an experience that many are longing for in the Arab world.

As I was writing these words, a chief officer called desiring one thing: That I would pray for him. Most requests that arrive on my desk are prayer requests. In our services, we have often shortened our sermons in order to give people more opportunity to come forward for prayer. Prayer should be at the heart of our services and ministries: prayers of thanksgiving, of blessing and of opportunities and prayers for invitations for more people to come to God through Jesus Christ.

Prayer is a powerful tool that brings amazing transformation in the lives of our community, yet we seldom use it. The time has come to pray more fervently for our people and teach them to do the same.

12

Belonging

In the Arab and North African worlds, there is a trend for emerging churches or life groups to separate themselves from the mother church or the institutional church. Some do it for security reasons and out of fear, others do not want to be associated with the institutional church and its history, and still others do it because they want greater autonomy. But there is a danger that such groups will drift away from key Christian doctrines or even fall under abusive leaders. The accumulated wisdom of the church throughout the ages needs continuously to inform, guide and protect individuals from going astray. That is why we stress the Scriptures, the creed, baptism and the Lord's Supper.

At the same time, the church has to listen carefully to the needs of the present generation, which are different from those of the previous generation, and continue to evolve in its presentation of the gospel (though not in its content). This constant dialogue between the church and individuals is essential if the church is not to become a historical museum and to prevent individuals from detaching themselves from the rich relational and spiritual experience that comes from belonging to the church community.

In this chapter, we will begin by looking at the features that sociologists have identified as essential to the existence of a community, and then we will look at some issues that we have found to be important when Muslim-background believers join Christ's body.

What Makes a Community?

Sociologists have recognized that all communities share certain cultural features. We will look briefly at each of these, and show how they apply to our church community.

A shared name

Every community has some way of referring to itself that is recognized by those inside the community and by those outside it. For example, World Vision and Youth for Christ are the names used by organizations, which are a form of community. In our case, we encourage people to identify themselves on the broadest level as followers of Jesus, but on the local level we want them to see themselves not as isolated believers but as members of the community that is known as Resurrection Church Beirut.

A shared history

Communities do not emerge out of nowhere. They all have a history of events and decisions that led to their formation and shape their continued existence. We can see this on a national level when we look at the Jews, whose thinking is deeply shaped by their history, going back as far as the exodus from Egypt. But even organizations and churches have a history. Understanding that history helps us to understand the shape of the community today, and to understand why certain decisions may be made or resisted. Introducing newcomers to some of that history will help them to understand where they fit in a greater whole.

A shared culture

All communities use a common language. This may or may not be everyone's mother tongue, but it is a language in which they can communicate with one another. They may also have developed an in-group vocabulary, which can be daunting to newcomers. The shared culture also includes a set of shared beliefs and values (as in the Yazidi community in Iraq) and a shared set of symbols. These symbols become boundary markers and identity signs for members of the community. In fact it has been said that one way to learn about a community or organization is to examine the symbols it uses.

To illustrate what I mean, we can look at the Jews in Jesus's day. For them, the temple in Jerusalem was a symbol of God's dwelling among his people, the land was a symbol of his generous care for them, and the Torah was the symbol of God's covenant and promises. So they gathered for worship at the temple and studied the Torah to discern God's will and purpose. The Gentiles in Jesus's day had their own symbols – they had their temples, their sacrificial system, their statues, coinage, stadiums and theatres. The early church did not identify with the Gentile symbols, and they replaced the Jewish symbols with Christ-centered symbols. Jesus becomes the true temple where both Jews and Gentiles meet God. The ethnic Jewish nation is radically redefined by a body drawn from every tribe, people, nation and tongue, namely, the body of Christ, the church. The focus thus shifts from the physical ownership of land to the kingdom of God. One ethnic group can claim a specific piece of land, but when the church comes from every tongue, tribe, nation and people, the whole world becomes the promised land, for where Christ dwells, there is the promised land.

In the church, Christ is all in all, and adhering to him is the marker that one is part of this new community. His cross becomes a symbol of life, salvation, redemption, and sanctification. His body, the church, becomes a symbol of the new creation. Mission becomes a symbol of obedience to Christ and a public confession that Christ, rather than any political authority, is Lord of all. Anyone who wants to belong to this community has to embrace Christ, his life, his crucifixion (he is Savior of the world), his resurrection and exaltation (He is Lord over all) and his body (the church), the multi-faceted symbol of this new community.

No one who rejects the Jesus revealed in the New Testament can belong to this community. One cannot just accept the parts of the New Testament one likes and dismiss the rest. One cannot reject the cross and retain Jesus's ethics and be part of this new community. One cannot reject the lordship of Christ and keep the cross. Someone said it in this way: "Christ is either Lord of all or not lord at all."

These are the key symbols required for belonging to the church of Christ in general, and for membership in the RCB community.

Community, Identity and Theology

Certain elements of our Christian identity are not negotiable, but others are cultural. There are also Christians who want to retain elements of their previous identity before they chose to follow Christ. They may find themselves experiencing a conflict between their Christian identity and their cultural identity. It is important that such issues be addressed if people are to have a sense of belonging to the body of Christ, rather than merely being outsiders observing it.

Not every aspect of our previous identity has to be discarded. We as leaders must take great care to be sensitive in our actions and reactions to cultural symbols. Rather than responding hastily, we should pay attention to the person's motive for retaining them. This may mean that we will have very different responses to the same symbol in different contexts. What I mean will become clear in the examples that follow. But before going on to look at specific examples, we can look at what Paul had to say when writing to a multi-ethnic church in Galatia about the identity-based conflicts they were experiencing.

Primary and secondary identities

Paul began by stressing that the Galatians' Christian identity was now their primary identity – they were all children of God through faith in Christ Jesus (Gal 3:26). So when conflicts arise, we too should encourage people not to say, "I am a child of God" but rather to say "I am one of the children of God."

In Christ, we are all equal. There is no superiority or priority, no question of social class or even gender – men and women have an equal status in Christ (Gal 3:28). In saying this, Paul is not dismissing a person's past and cultural identity. The categories he lists still existed, but they had all become relativized in the light of this new reality. In Christ, genuine equality happens with differences and not without them. Christ does not demolish our differences, but they become secondary to our primary identity as people who are in Christ. As such, we are all on the same level. Anyone who chooses to follow Jesus, whether from a Christian, Muslim, atheist or any other background, has to shift their identity, understand their new identity in Christ and live accordingly within the community of faith.

That being said, Paul was also prepared to adopt certain secondary identities if that became necessary to reach people for Christ. He discusses this at length in 1 Corinthians 9:19–23. At certain times, he would abide by Jewish customs; at others time he would live as a Gentile. As he put it, he was prepared to become "all things to all people, that by all means I might save some" (1 Cor 9:22). His goal in embracing cultural norms and lifestyles was not to water down his Christian identity but to proclaim Christ more powerfully in order to win more souls for the kingdom.

Note that the concept of freedom ran in both directions for Paul. He was not only free from those who imposed Jewish practices such as circumcision and other rituals on new believers, he was also free from those who tried to forbid believers from embracing those and other social norms. Paul saw no problem in abandoning Jewish rituals, regulations and ceremonies, yet he was willing to circumcise Timothy for the sake of the gospel. In our present context, he would reject both imposing or forbidding followers of Jesus from wearing the hijab. Each individual has the freedom and the responsibility to act in love in order to proclaim Christ in their own context and in the best way possible.

Paul was willing to do all this for the sake of the gospel, in order to proclaim, take part in, reflect the nature of and rejoice in the good news of Jesus becoming one of us (1 Cor 9:23). He was willing to relinquish his social rights, and become united with the other, while still preserving his identity in Christ, just as Jesus chose to unite himself with us without abandoning his identity as the Son of God.

Identity issues in the church

While we may acknowledge that we are all one in Christ, there can still sometimes be problems when different cultures come together in the same church. Paul addressed this point when writing to the church in Rome. It too was a multicultural congregation, made up of both Jews and non-Jews. The Jewish believers preserved their Jewish distinctiveness because they saw Christianity as a branch of Judaism. They argued that Christians should preserve and practise Jewish rituals and regulations as a sign that they belong to God's covenant people. The non-Jewish believers argued that the gospel transcends Jewish particularities and that God accepts us unconditionally, regardless of our background.

We have had somewhat similar problems in our churches in Lebanon where there are marked cultural differences between Christians from different regions and backgrounds. So we have had to learn to apply the principles Paul lays out for handling such disagreements in Romans 14:1–12.

Accept the weak without passing judgement on their opinions (Rom 14:1). Here "the weak" are the Christians who come from a Jewish background, for whom Jewish practices were an expression of their identity. They would feel that they were betraying God's covenant if they stopped observing them. Paul says that their position is to be accepted in the church.

Accept the strong without passing judgement on them. Acceptance goes both ways. Those with a Jewish background also had to accept the views of "the strong," those who were not Jewish. Paul gives two reasons for doing this: First, God has accepted the non-Jews into his family, and second, a Christian from a non-Jewish background is not inferior or a servant to a Christian from a Jewish background. In using their freedom, these Christians are also glorifying Christ (Rom 14:3–4).

Invite everyone to grow and mature. Instead of passing judgement on each other, everyone should work on growing in their own faith and seeking a clear understanding of what was right for them to do (Rom 1:5).

Encourage everyone to focus on the goal of glorifying Christ. What is important is not unified practice but a unified goal. Whether we observe a specific day or not, whether we eat a specific kind of food or not, what matters is the ultimate goal of doing everything for the Lord and for his glory (Rom 1:6).

Remind both groups that Christ rules over them and that he is the one they will all have to explain themselves to. God is the judge; we are not. We should live in the present in light of the coming day of judgement and be responsible for our own actions, not for the actions of others (Rom 1:9–13).

What do these principles mean in the context of a church with many Muslim-background believers? At minimum they mean that the "strong" (whoever the strong might be) should not despise the "weak." People should have a measure of freedom to practise what they think is vital for them without unhealthy pressure or coercion.

Second, the "weak" should not judge or condemn the "strong." In our context, the weak may be people with a Christian background who want to uphold specific church practices, or they may be people from a Muslim background who want to maintain strong cultural norms in a predominantly Muslim Arab society. We should all accept one another because God in Christ has accepted all of us.

Third, all groups should strive to grow and mature in light of the Scriptures, and none should claim full knowledge or exclusive truth. We need a learning spirit among us.

Fourth, whether people fast during Ramadan or not, wear a hijab or not, prostrate themselves, clap, stand still or dance, whether they ask to be buried in a Christian or non-Christian cemetery, what matters to Paul is the motive and the purpose. If the motive and purpose are to glorify Christ, let it be.

RCB provides many examples of how this works out in practice. Unbelievers from a Christian background who were invited to an event have glorified Christ when they saw believers from Muslim backgrounds wearing the hijab yet praising and worshiping Christ. On a different occasion, believers from a Christian background were encouraged and praised God when they saw believers from Muslim backgrounds who had experienced freedom in Christ decide to take off their hijabs during worship. These two responses may seem contradictory, but both brought glory to Christ. What matters is the motive and the purpose.

It is the same with baptism. When Muslims willingly choose to get baptized, they are praising Christ through their actions. Sometimes, however, Muslim women choose to postpone their baptisms in order to first win their spouses.

Their goal is also to glorify Christ, and the "strong" should not condemn the "weak" for not taking a bold decision to get baptized straightaway.

Some specific issues

Believers from both Muslim and Christian backgrounds will ultimately have to give an account to the living God for all they have done on this earth. So let us all walk in humility, with repenting souls and loving hearts, while seeking his mercy and grace daily until his return.

Dress codes

Some people in the West react strongly when they see a woman wearing a hijab (head covering). So I am sometimes asked whether we allow women to wear head coverings at church. My response is that people are free to preserve their cultural identity, provided they do so in Christ. Thus when it comes to the dress code at RCB, this is a matter of freedom. People can come as they are to the church without borrowing other people's cultural dress codes. So some dress in a modern way, others dress in a traditional way, and some women wear the hijab while others do not.

Sometimes new believers come to me and ask whether they should keep wearing the hijab or take it off. There is no simple "yes" or "no" answer to this question. Normally, I respond by asking them, "Why do you want to take it off (or keep it on)?" Some answer that they want to keep wearing it as a sign that they respect and honor their husband and his family. Others say that they would feel naked and uncomfortable if their head were uncovered. Still others say they want to continue to wear the hijab because they want to be a blessing in their community. In all these cases, my response would be that of course they are free to keep wearing it. Other women want to take off the hijab as a sign of the freedom they have in Christ. Their choice too should be respected.

I have, however, had a few cases where female believers from a Muslim background tell me they don't want to take off their head covering because they feel they are sinning by doing so (or that God will punish them if they do). In this instance, they need to be shown who God is, understand that there is freedom in Christ, and taught what sin is and is not.

Another new believer might say that she needs to keep wearing the hijab because it is prescribed in the Muslim tradition recorded in the Hadith and so she must wear it. Here we need to ensure that we teach new believers that their ultimate authority is Christ as revealed in the Scriptures, and that we are not bound by other traditions.

Someone else may say, I want to keep the hijab because it reflects my Islamic identity. In that case, my follow-up question would be: "Do you mean your cultural identity or your religious identity?" Depending on the answer, the discussion might take different directions. Sometimes it is hard to differentiate between the two.

The goal of our advice is always to encourage new believers to grow in Christ. Slowly life-in-Christ will become their criterion for accepting, rejecting or transforming cultural norms.

Reading the Qur'an

As I have said earlier, we encourage all who attend RCB to study the Scriptures. But sometimes someone will tell me that they would like to read the Qur'an, and ask me whether it would be wrong for them to do this. Once again, it is important to ask the "why" question before responding. So I ask, "Why do you want to read the Qur'an? Is it in order to understand your neighbor or is it because you believe that it is the word of God?" If your goal is to serve your community better and be more sensitive in your daily relationships with others, then this is a great start.

Going to the mosque on Friday

Similar questions need to be asked if someone wishes to attend the mosque on Friday. There is nothing wrong with going to the mosque. You can pray to Jesus there and be a great witness. However, is your visit to a mosque seen as a threat by others? Does it create tension in your community? Does it cause more misunderstanding? Do people think you are a hypocrite? Your answer to those questions may guide you as to how you should act.

Maintaining family relationships

Sometimes, Muslim-background believers ask how they can grow in maturity in Christ while retaining a good relationship with their Muslim families. This is possible, and depending on the level of persecution, a person can discern how open they can be to their family. Believers from Christian backgrounds stay connected to their relatives and friends and continue to love and serve their families, and so should believers from a Muslim background. Yet they should recognize that their social identity (as a Muslim), though still important, now takes second place to their new identity in Christ.

Naming and raising children

Names still matter in the Arab world. They are important clues to identity. Thus while some Muslim-background believers give their children new Christian names, others prefer their children to have Muslim names to avoid drawing attention to their Christian faith. This is especially the case when the children are enrolled in schools with a Muslim majority.

Normally, people can tell from someone's habits, words, clothing, and actions what religion they adhere to – or they may ask them about it outright. So children whose names disguise their religion may have a sense of leading a double life. This is not healthy for children, or for any of us. So it may sometimes be easier for the children of believers if they attend Christian schools, where they can behave, act and speak as Christians. But this option is not open to all parents.

Marrying

I have left this issue till last because it is in many ways the most complex. Pastors in the West may be accustomed to advising Christians not to marry non-Christians and leaving it at that. But while that principle is valid, it is inadequate when it comes to addressing marriage in the Arab world or in Arab communities elsewhere in the world. Here marriage is not seen as an individual matter but as involving whole communities. There are many regions of the Arab world where it is almost impossible for a Christian-background believer to marry a Muslim-background believer. So when it comes to marriage, the best way logistically is for a Muslim-background believer to marry another Muslim-background believer. They can marry legally at a sheikh's office, and then they can have a public or a private marriage ceremony at church afterwards.

In Lebanon, however, it is possible to change one's religious identity. A Muslim can become a Christian, and vice versa. Muslim converts can change their religious identity and get married, and their children will be assumed to be following the father's religion.

As a pastor in a multi-ethnic church in Lebanon, I have come across many possible combinations when it comes to marriage. Each combination presents special challenges that a pastor who offers premarital counselling needs to be aware of and prepare the couple to face. To give you an idea of what I mean, here are sixteen different combinations we have come across. You may do well to read them and not gloss over them, especially if your church has an extensive ministry to refugees and immigrants:

1. *A man and woman of a similar religious background, similar Christian commitment, similar church affiliation, similar nationality.* These

two believers share the same background and grew up in the same church. Premarital counselling is still important, but this new family faces no unusual struggles or uncommon persecution.

2.   *A man and woman of a similar religious background, similar Christian commitment, similar church affiliation, different nationality.* This combination is becoming very common as the world becomes smaller. Moreover, churches with partnerships and good connections with other national churches experience more and more of this phenomenon (short-term mission teams play into it too). For example, a German man who works in a Christian organization got to know one of our woman leaders. They married and moved to Germany. This type of marriage presents a challenge to local churches as they lose key leaders through "matrimonial migration." On the other hand, a Venezuelan female believer met a Christian Lebanese leader in our church. They got married and stayed to serve in Lebanon. Premarital and cross-cultural counselling are important for all such couples.

3.   *A man and woman of a similar religious background, similar Christian commitment, different church affiliation, similar nationality.* This is another common case, and the further apart the churches are doctrinally, the harder it becomes – especially on the church. A believer from a Baptist background may fairly easily marry a believer from a Pentecostal background, especially if the Baptist church is not cessationist in its theology (that is, believing that spiritual gifts ceased with the apostolic age). Things get more complicated when a Catholic believer marries an evangelical believer, particularly when they have children. For Catholics, infant baptism is not only a religious duty but a family identity stamp, and when one of the spouses refuses to accept it, it can create friction in the family. Disagreement about which church the parents or the children should attend can also affect the spiritual health of the family and create real tension if these matters are not well communicated and agreed upon before marriage. Yet the couple's mutual faith in Christ, their daily devotion, and their commitment to one another can help them to make it through.

4.   *A man and woman of a similar religious background, similar Christian commitment, different church affiliation, different nationality.* This couple faces similar challenges to the third group above, but with the

additional problem of different cultural backgrounds. There is plenty of scope for miscommunication if both partners speak different languages and they chose to speak a third common language (say, English). But if they are intentional about communicating effectively, they can learn more about each other's differences than a couple of the same nationality.

5. *A man and woman of a similar religious background, no Christian commitment, similar church affiliation, similar nationality.* Many Lebanese people with strong church affiliation do not have a real commitment to following Jesus. They consider themselves nominal Christians (or are perceived by others as such), but nonetheless feel attached to their denomination even though they never or only occasionally visit the church (mainly for weddings, funerals or baptisms). Nominal Christian families in Lebanon are going through major challenges and the number of divorces is rapidly increasing. In a culture of honor and shame, this rarely happened in the past, for people would endure unhappy marriages rather than seeking divorce and being shunned by the community. Nowadays, a sense of justice is prevailing. Spouses who feel betrayed or abused are refusing to maintain the status quo and are walking out on their marriages.

6. *A man and woman of a similar religious background, no Christian commitment, different church affiliation, similar nationality.* This couple is in much the same position as the previous one. These days, it is quite common to have married couples coming from two different church affiliations, and it causes fewer challenges than we used to see in the past. However, an older Orthodox priest may confront a woman about choosing to marry a Catholic man, or he may confront an Orthodox man who wants to marry a female who attends an evangelical church. But it seems that such pressure often merely increases the couple's determination to marry. After all, Lebanese law does allow for cross-religious and cross-denominational marriages.

7. *A man and woman of a similar religious background, no Christian commitment, similar church affiliation, different nationality.* This couple will face that same challenges faced by #5 above, especially when they have a similar religious background.

8. *A man and woman of a similar religious background, no Christian commitment, different church affiliation, different nationality.* This couple will face the same challenges faced by #6.

9. *A man and woman of a different religious background, similar Christian commitment, similar church affiliation, similar nationality.* Here we are talking about two committed followers of Jesus, one from a Muslim or Druze background and the other from a Christian background. They attend the same church, and they are from the same country. If both are Lebanese, the Muslim-background spouse is allowed by law to change their religious status and become a Christian to get married in a church. However, in the Arab world in general, it is not possible to change your status from Muslim to Christian. It is almost impossible for a Christian man (let's say a Copt) to marry a Muslim-background believer (let's say a Sunni), unless he converts to Islam and gets married under Sharia law. If the man chooses not to convert (as is generally the case), he will need to travel to Cyprus or Turkey for a civil marriage and will need to live outside his home country since he will never be considered married there. An Egyptian couple in our church suffered for years from this unfair system. When the wife was found to be pregnant, they had to immigrate to Brazil in order to be able to register their child and legalize their situation. If, however, the man is of a Muslim background and the female is a Christian, things are much easier. According to Sharia law, a Muslim man may marry a Christian woman in their home country. Some such couples choose to have a church ceremony for the family and ask God's blessing on their marriage.

10. *A man and woman of a different religious background, similar Christian commitment, similar church affiliation, different nationality.* If one of the couple is Lebanese and the other is not, and is an Arab from a Muslim background, a Lebanese pastor cannot legally marry them. They will need to get married outside Lebanon.

11. *A man and woman of a different religious background, similar Christian commitment, different church affiliation, similar nationality.* See #3 and #9.

12. *A man and woman of a different religious background, similar Christian commitment, different church affiliation, different nationality.* See #10.

13. *A man and woman of a different religious background, no religious commitment, different church/mosque affiliation, same nationality.* See group #9. The counsellor or pastor who is marrying such a couple may have a wonderful opportunity to introduce them to Christ and invite them to learn what it means to live under the lordship of Christ in marriage.

14. *A man and woman of a different religious background, no religious commitment, different church/mosque affiliation, different nationality.* See #10.

15. *A man and woman of a different religious background, one spouse with a Christian commitment, different church/mosque affiliation, same nationality.* In counselling such couples, the pastor needs to be very clear about the challenges that they will face in the future. We have seen a case of a believer committed to his evangelical church who divorced his Christian wife to marry a Druze woman, whom he later divorced. He ended up walking away from following Jesus altogether.

16. *A man and woman of a different religious background, one spouse with a Christian commitment, having different church/mosque affiliation, different nationality.* Similar to #15. I have known a missionary working with a well-known evangelical mission organization who divorced his wife, married a Sunni non-believer and moved to an Arab country with her.

As you can see, we face many complex situations! More and more we are hearing stories of young men and women from different backgrounds falling in love with each other. The more different ethnic groups live together, the more likely such cross-cultural marriages are. Some parents will resist such marriages, but the more people (both parents and children) grow rooted in Christ, the easier it becomes to solve these cross-cultural challenges.

When two Muslim-background believers choose to get married, there tends to be less social and domestic upheaval than when one is from a Muslim and the other from a Christian background. However, as a church we encourage followers of Jesus to marry followers of Jesus regardless of their background, provided they have good marriage counselling and are willing to continue to work on their relationship.

To those who come to us and say that their parents want them to marry a Muslim who does not follow Jesus, we explain that the deepest connection between two people is spiritual. If they wish to live for Christ fully, raise their children in the Lord, and belong to the community of his followers, they need to challenge their parents' wishes, although this may cause persecution. Ideally, focusing on inviting whole families to follow Jesus can prevent such clashes.

Conclusion

If someone coming to Christ from a Muslim background wants to retain cultural norms compatible with the word of God, then I suggest that person can truly say, "I am a Muslim follower of Jesus." By saying this they mean that their social and cultural status is Muslim, but their religious and spiritual status is rooted in Christ. I think that Paul would agree.

Diversity in the non-essentials is richness in Christianity, and it is to be welcomed. The old saying, "In essentials, unity; in non-essentials, liberty; and in all things, charity" is certainly valid today.

13

Structuring

With the influx of Syrians and Iraqis adding to the diversity already present in Lebanon, our church has learned – and is still learning – how to create real community among those of multi-ethnic and multi-religious backgrounds. Worshiping together (through congregational worship), doing life together (through small groups with friends, neighbors and colleagues) and growing in a healthy spiritual family (whether the small unit of husband and wife or the bigger unit that includes grandparents, uncles, aunts, cousins, etc.) are key to spiritual maturity and an effective Christian presence in the Middle East. It is through these three communities that we mature in grace and holiness, serve our community more holistically, and impact a larger group of people with the power of the gospel. The church that thus stands in continuity with the early church plays a crucial role in resisting unhealthy Western individualism by stressing the importance of belonging to a wider body and submitting to a greater wisdom led by the Spirit of God.

But it is all too easy for a church to fail at its task, become disunited and cease to be a community. Sometimes the reason for such failure lies with the members of the church, but at other times, the problems are exacerbated by the fact that the church has grown larger than was ever anticipated. So in this chapter we will be talking about how we at RCB have tried to cope with the explosive growth of our church through the church culture we have tried to nurture and the organizational structures we have put in place.

To give you an idea of the scope of our problem, RCB now has three campuses and we are planting a number of churches in the region. On our main campus, we hold three services every Sunday, and people can choose which service to attend. This gives them freedom to go where they feel most comfortable. Although all services are open to all, some people choose to attend services where others of a similar background are present. Refugees with no cars come together on buses (sometimes provided by the church) and this logistically clusters them together in one service.

To retain our unity as a church, we have found it vital that we not only define what we believe (which has already been discussed in the chapter on teaching) but also define and actively promote our core values as a church. We have also tried to set up organizational structures that, while not excessively controlling, do not allow total autonomy without accountability.

Church Values

When we speak of church culture (or organizational culture) what we are referring to is a specific community's way of organizing itself. As was pointed out earlier, all communities have a shared history, use shared language and symbols, have a set of shared beliefs and values, and are united around a shared mission and vision. In our case, our mission is to proclaim Jesus to all and to train those who follow him to live as his disciples. Our history (or some of it) has been told in this book. Our language and symbolism are rooted in the Bible. So are our values in the broadest sense. But organization theorists have pointed out that every organization (and thus also every church) has its own particular subset of values.

Categories of values

It is possible to identify four different categories of values in any organization:[1]

- *Core values* are inherent in an organization. These values already exist; they are not hoped for. They are part of the organization's identity. One good way to identify the core values in a church is to look at the people who are most admired in the congregation. What is it about their behavior that makes them loved and admired by others? The answer to that question may reveal a core value. You could also try looking at the people in the congregation who are considered "difficult" and asking what is it about their behavior that makes others feel uncomfortable around them? Is it that words and actions contradict some core value in the group? In RCB, our core values are honor, loving one another, a spirit of servanthood and

---

1. Patrick Lencioni, *The Advantage: Why Organizational Health Trumps Everything Else in Business* (San Francisco: Jossey-Bass, 2012), 91–104.

a spirit of joy. These core values must not be taken for granted but must be actively nurtured.

- *Aspirational values* are not inherent within an organization and should be purposefully inserted into its culture. For instance, at RCB we constantly try to encourage teamwork, accountability and effective communication, values that are not necessarily part of our Arab culture. We have even adjusted our organizational structure to promote these values.

- *Permission-to-play values* are "the minimum behavioral standards that are required in an organization." I would say that in a church context, honesty is a permission-to-play value.

- *Accidental values* are values that are evident in an organization but came about unintentionally and might not necessarily serve the good of the organization. For instance, dependability has become an accidental value at RCB. Refugees who lack almost everything rely on the church to help them, but unless the church develops creative projects to help refugees become (to some extent) self-sustaining, dependability can create dependency, which harms both the church and the refugee community in the long run.

This is not the place to explain all of our church's core values in detail, but I do want to explore one of our core values further, to show how deeply it affects all that we are and do.

Honor

Honor is a biblical value. We honor our leaders, we honor our parents, we honor those who work hard among us, and as Christians we honor all human beings because they are created in the image of God, regardless of their ethnic or religious background. Children, women and men all deserve our honor and respect. But, especially in the Arab world, we seldom see leaders honoring other leaders. It happens, but rarely. Leaders like to take the glory for themselves. This reflects our sinful humanity, and it is something we must combat.

Note that honoring our leaders is not the same as worshiping them. Sadly, in some circles, people "worship" the leader, the president, the rich, the pastor, or the priest. Such worship is not only wrong because it is directed to another human being but also because it is directed to only one person, namely the one on the top. True honor is shown in a culture in which *all* are honored. This kind of honor is mutual. It is vertical and horizontal, and operates in all other directions.

Honor is not blind submission to the leadership; rather, honor is a daily acknowledgement, privately and publicly, that our leaders are sacrificially giving their lives to help us grow to maturity. It is also an acknowledgement that without the least in the congregation, we would not be where we are today. A leader is made great by his congregation. A congregation thrives by its leaders. We honor our leaders when we listen to them, and leaders honor their congregations when they listen to them and their needs. When we hear and retain *who* said something, and give them credit, this is honor. I am learning on a daily basis to honor and give credit to others.

Moreover, honor also includes the dead and the unborn. The dead are our predecessors who have left us a great legacy. Yet I have seen leaders neglect the past because it is inconsistent with what they believe today. That is a waste of energy and time. Disruptive leadership does not build a great organization. Every past has great and valuable lessons to learn from, as well as mistakes to avoid. I have discovered that the more I study the past, the fewer mistakes I make. We should also honor the unborn. We honor them by striving to leave a faithful and fruitful church for the next generation.

Living with a culture of honor calls for developing a character of humility and security. We Arabs tend to be proud and insecure, but there is hope in Christ in our midst.

At RCB we have developed a model of honor that has transformed our relationships. It shows (1) how the leader honors team members, (2) how the team members honor their leader, and (3) how team members honor one another.

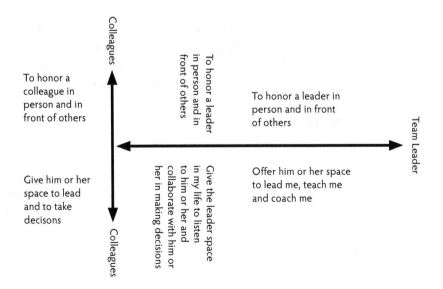

Honoring people also means that we honor their culture and beliefs. This does not necessarily mean that we agree with their beliefs, but it does mean that we respect them and what they stand for. We can speak gently against wrong beliefs, and we can critique people's arguments, but this should always be done with love and respect. This value means that when people come to us, we not only allow them to maintain their cultural norms and lifestyle but we also encourage it, providing it does not deviate from the teaching of Jesus. This culture of honor allows Syrians, Iraqis and Lebanese alike to enter our churches and feel respected and welcomed. I believe everyone likes to be part of an honoring culture. Muslims will feel understood and nurtured in this context, and believers from a Christian background will not feel abused and taken advantage of.

You cannot be suspicious of or hostile towards someone you honor. Some newcomers do feel suspicious about certain individuals and ethnic groups, but this feeling rapidly evaporates when they discover the honoring culture they have walked into, as well as observing the example of honor demonstrated by the leaders. When conflict does occur, it can be used as an opportunity to re-affirm our core values and what we stand for. When misunderstanding happens and gets resolved, it bonds people together.

Life groups are one way of honoring people and their culture within a smaller setting, where individuals of similar cultural backgrounds can cherish their culture and feel comfortable and accepted by others.

Church Structure

In order to flourish and be fruitful, churches need strong governance and a healthy structure. There are many possible governance models, and I cannot discuss them all here. What I will do is present some of the points we considered when setting up our own structures at RCB, and encourage you to take these into account in your church.

Structure should focus on people

Whatever structure is adopted, it should focus on people first. As Jim Collins puts it, the "who" should come before the "what."[2] His key point is that before we talk about vision, strategy, and tactics, we should think about "who" we

---

2. Jim Collins, *Good to Great: Why Some Companies Make the Leap . . . and Others Don't* (New York: HarperCollins, 2001), 41–64.

are working with and for. This point may seem obvious, but such thinking is still uncommon in many places. I have seen many leaders come up with ideas for ministries and then start searching their congregations for people to carry them out. When they can't find people equipped and called to execute their ideas, mediocrity and frustration often follow. One of the reasons RCB grew was that we started with the "who." When we discovered that we had a group of people at RCB who were eager to serve the marginalized, we began to serve Syrian workers in our neighborhood. This happened just before the start of the civil war in Syria in 2012. When refugees started to flow into Lebanon, RCB was ready to host and serve the refugee community. To give another example, God brought men and women to RCB who are skilled in production and filming, so we started to serve congressmen and other leaders by producing short videos to promote ethical and social initiatives for the good of the nation.

Structure should empower people

In the Arab world, churches tend to revolve around one leader who controls what is done. This is seldom healthy. Leaders should focus more on equipping and leading people and less on doing things for them, for people grow when they serve. A church will not grow if the congregation expect the staff to do everything while they simply enjoy what the staff offer. The staff should equip the congregation to serve and grow by giving them time, resources and skills in ministry.

Structure should include checks and balances

Checks and balances are good ways of creating accountability, but are uncommon in the Arab world. In a culture that focuses on honor and shame, people may feel threatened, under scrutiny or mistrusted when we set them up. So while systems of accountability are necessary, they need to be put in place within a context of trust.

In the early stages of church growth, it may be difficult to implement such a structure. But as the church grows, a strong board of elders, a visionary pastor, an effective staff team, a well-structured volunteer group and a committed body of believers are vital in order to carry out the mission. The structure should allow for creative visions to be cast, fleshed out, and evaluated; for talents to surface and be used with a great degree of autonomy as well as harmony; for strategic plans to be executed within clear time frames; and for evaluation, critique, problem-solving and improvement to take place on a regular basis.

Structure should protect the weak

The church leadership and any established structure should always protect the marginalized from abuse and exploitation. The weak, the broken, refugees and the impoverished are vulnerable and so are open to abuse. Sometimes the abusers are not even aware of what they are doing. For example, it may be unfair to expect people in these circumstances to attend many meetings, receive Western donors in their modest homes, and be involved in ministries, or even to insist that they attend Sunday morning services. We all know that we should not exploit the needy. But rarely do we hear leaders raising their voice against manipulative attitudes and schemes that take advantage of the kindness and charity they are shown. Abuse may even extend to the leadership; there are some leaders with great hearts and compassion who feel strangled by the unending demands made on them and end up neglecting their families.

Structure should include financial accountability

The local church should create a stable financial structure so that main ministries are not threatened when donations are low, and so that ministries can expand in times of abundance. We should not only encourage people to give but should also communicate the needs of the congregation and how our money is being spent. For instance, in a church where 70 percent of the members are refugees who lack basics such as food, it is hard for the other 30 percent to cater for everyone's needs. In such cases, any attempt to seek funding from outside sources should be the outcome of a close and deep relationship between some partners and the local church, and the leaders should be in agreement about the direction in which they are taking the church. Failure to reach such agreement results in the type of misunderstanding, frustration and mistrust that split a church in Lebanon when its pastor secured large sums of money to help with the refugee crisis but the leaders of the church disagreed with his approach.

Church Leader

In an earlier chapter, I spoke about the need to have a multi-ethnic leadership team, and in this chapter I have already spoken of how the value of honoring one another should shape the church leadership team. So at this point I will merely address the skills that are needed by a senior pastor leading a large multi-ethnic church. Ideally, such a person should be able to fulfil the requirements of the following three roles:

- *Leader*. Leaders can see beyond the present and are able to envision where they want the church to be twenty years down the road. They can communicate this vision to others and lead leaders working to bring it about. They are also capable of discerning looming storms and courageous enough to ride their waves. Senior pastors who are far stronger in this dimension than in the other two need to be able to find helpers who are shepherds and managers and empower them to complement them in their role.

- *Shepherd*. Shepherds have big hearts and can feel the burden of their people. They cry and rejoice with them. Such pastors are like fathers to their churches. However, if such a pastor does not also have management skills, their congregations are unlikely to grow beyond 100 to 120 members. Moreover, pastors who are shepherds also need to show courageous leadership if their churches are not to suffer paralysis.

- *Manager*. Managers can develop leaders and allow things to happen. Managers are good maximizers and great believers in people, but they can hurt many along the way. Administrators who are good at managing projects but poor at managing people should never become pastors.

Someone who is simultaneously a leader, a shepherd and a manager is an exceptional senior pastor. Such people are not common. In the Arab world, I have found that most pastors are only shepherding their churches, not leading them. This is one of the reasons why our churches do not grow.

Jesus was a great leader, who had a kingdom vision; he was able to see the cross when no one in the Jewish or the Hellenistic world could fathom it, and he was courageous to see it through for our sake. Moreover, Jesus was the true Shepherd, who was moved with great compassion towards the needy and broken. Finally, Jesus was the one who called his disciples, trained them and empowered them to lead his mission during his life on earth and after his ascension. He managed his disciples so that they could execute his vision. He is our role model in leadership.

14

Suffering

It has been said that "a cross-centered gospel requires cross-carrying messengers."[1] That is certainly what Christ meant when he said, "If anyone would come after me, let him deny himself and take up his cross daily and follow me" (Luke 9:23). This does not sound optional to me. Paul followed in Jesus's footsteps, and could write "I have been crucified with Christ. It is no longer I who live, but Christ who lives in me" (Gal 2:20).

Following Christ is costly. Jesus warned that some would kill us while thinking that they were offering service to God (John 16:33). Persecution is the norm for followers of Christ. The ties between discipleship and persecution are so strong in the Scriptures that it seems unavoidable. This new way of life to which we call people includes a daily invitation to join Christ in carrying the cross. Those who examine the book of Revelation understand that God conquered the world not by sending a lion (as the Jews expected), but by sending a lamb to be slaughtered for the sins of the world.

Experiencing Persecution

When we celebrate incarnational living, as we did in the first part of this book, we should also remember that we need to celebrate incarnational dying as well. Look again at Paul's great hymn to Christ:

> Have this mind among yourselves, which is yours in Christ Jesus, who, though he was in the form of God, did not count equality with God a thing to be grasped, but emptied himself, by taking the form of a servant, being born in the likeness of men. And being

---

1. Glenn Penner, *In the Shadow of the Cross: A Biblical Theology of Persecution and Discipleship* (2004), quoted in Don Little, *Effective Discipling in Muslim Communities* (Downers Grove: InterVarsity Press, 2015), 213.

found in human form, he humbled himself by becoming obedient
to the point of death, even death on a cross. (Phil 2:5–8)

Like him, we are called to follow a path of suffering, humiliation and love. This truth is well known in the Middle East where persecution can come from all directions: from the government, from militant groups, from the extended family, and from a brother or spouse. I recently sat separately with one couple and two individuals who have been following Jesus for more than two years, and they shared with me about their everyday lives. The issue for them was not whether they would suffer persecution, but how they were to manage their lives in the midst of it. Persecution is very real and sadly, their experience is not uncommon among our brothers and sisters.

What form does persecution take in our context? Below are a few examples of what members of our congregation have experienced:

- Attempts to kill someone who is regarded as apostate.
- Phone calls from a brother or a close relative threatening to kill a woman because she is shaming the family. (Fortunately, few carry out that threat, but the threat is real.)
- Phone calls from close relatives disowning a believing woman. Her WhatsApp messages may be blocked, and when she calls her family, no one picks up the phone.
- Marginalization and exclusion from weddings and funerals.
- Taking away a woman's children.
- Being forced to sit with her husband and read the Qur'an.
- Being forced to wear a hijab.
- Physical and sexual abuse.
- Detention at home, with the wife and child being forbidden to leave the house or go to church.
- Abandonment, with the husband marrying another woman without divorcing his believing wife in order to increase her affliction.
- Job loss because of their faith.
- Exclusion from job opportunities or unfair pay.
- Financial persecution, including the loss of an inheritance or a monthly allowance.
- Prohibiting believers from meeting regularly with other believers.

Those are the cases I have come across in my own church. I have also heard from the head of an NGO about a Muslim Syrian woman who became an outcast and was kicked out of her house and her village because she married a Christian. (The leader of the NGO found her and took her in.) There is also the horrific story of Sara Fatima Al-Mutairi's murder by her brother because she became a Christian. She was only twenty-six years of age when her brother burnt her face, tortured her and killed her because she followed Jesus. In her letter to Magy al-Khoury she wrote:

> I was searching about the truthfulness of the Gospels and of Jesus because I was greatly attracted to Jesus. From the very beginning when I started reading about him I saw the difference between what I believed about Mohammad and what I was discovering about Jesus in the Gospels . . . What really attracts me in the Gospels is the story of Jesus. In my view, this is the greatest story in human history. It is the best example of love, redemption and humility.[2]

Fatima had to pay a high price for choosing to follow Jesus; others will too, until God fully establishes his kingdom on earth. The West sees following Jesus as a form of entertainment. Yes, there is plenty of joy and peace in Christ, but, in our region and during the first few centuries of Christianity, it was always coupled with persecution and suffering.

Persecution can either come from the authorities, from the community in general, or from close family. When people are displaced, persecution is reduced. When families move outside their communities, they are less known in their new settings.

We need to be aware that the use of the media can escalate persecution. We know of cases where believers from a non-Christian background have recorded their testimonies hoping for some financial return and this has increased their persecution. Although the recorded testimonies are accurate and the hearing of such testimonies probably does strengthen the faith of others, especially in places where authorities use fear to control and intimidate seekers, the families of those who recorded their stories were almost always put in difficult situations due to the shame and dishonor associated with a family member becoming a Christian.

Minimizing Persecution

How do new believers respond to the threat of persecution? How do they respond when they face the threat of losing members of their families, parts

---

2. http://ibrahim-al-copti.blogspot.com/2008/09/blog- post_4701.html.

of their body, their jobs, friends, place of worship, their home, access to good water and food, and peace of mind?

Our advice is not to promise new believers a life where persecution is absent but to instruct them in how to avoid unnecessary persecution, how to have a long-term impact on their families first and then on their neighborhood, how to stay connected culturally and not to look or sound "weird," and how to seize every opportunity to share Christ through deeds and words, and not through religiousness. Jesus is welcome in most places in the Arab world. He is the key not only to hearts but to our Arab culture and to different communities.

We have noticed that immediately after their conversion men tend to become more passionate and may sound quite aggressive. For example, one man who has been coming to our church for at least two years told me that he had five Qur'ans and had decided to throw them all in the trash. This was quite surprising to me as the senior pastor of a church that always preaches respect for other religions and their symbols.

When we ask these men why they are reacting so aggressively, we get answers like "Because we have been living a big lie," and "People need to wake up from this lie," and "I lost forty years of my life for nothing. I don't want my friends to have the same experience." Although their animosity towards their old religion can be explained psychologically, it is still startling for us as leaders who relentlessly try to demonstrate love in a practical way. How can you have such hatred now that you have seen a community that loves even its enemies and that reached out to you when you were among those "enemies"? The church needs to be ultra-cautious when dealing with such emotions lest people get trapped by the snares of the old god of hatred while still at the threshold of the kingdom of love.

Women, on the other hand, generally do not turn aggressive when they come to Christ. They do, however, become more confident and inwardly secure, and they cultivate discernment and develop wisdom and insight. In order not to lose their children and spouse, they become thoughtful about what and when and with whom they share their new faith. Many women choose not to do so openly to their spouses immediately after their conversion. They prepare the way by their good deeds, until their husbands, seeing the transformation, ask for the reason, and then the believing spouse opens up to share her faith in Christ. One woman told me, "I don't tell my husband what to do; instead I come to him asking him to explain a verse from the Bible to me. I then read the verse and I honor him by asking him to interpret it for me." I find this to be very respectful, honoring and empowering. She is inviting him to study the word of God without putting him in the uncomfortable and culturally intimidating situation of feeling that he is being taught by his wife. Other women choose to keep wearing a hijab as an honoring gesture and an indirect message that following Jesus is not an invitation to live a rebellious life or to become a rebellious spouse. Others have shared with us that their becoming better mothers encourages their husbands to keep allowing them to go to church and to prayer gatherings.

One woman told us that what drew her husband to Christ was the transformation he saw in her, especially in her relationship with her children. Although women rarely shout at their husbands in the Arab world, it is very common for mothers to instruct and correct their children through shouting and scolding. The peaceful home and the loving environment that new believing women create is a key foundation not just for the conversion of their husbands but for their husbands' permitting them to stay connected with their new Christ-following communities.

Leading in a Context of Persecution

Leaders who serve among people of non-Christian backgrounds should not take lightly the cost of serving Christ, especially if they are married and have children. Serving in the Arab world is life-threatening. I do not mean to say that it is life-threatening all the time, but the reality is that it can happen anytime. In Lebanon, we do have a great measure of freedom to share Christ with anyone. This, however, does not prevent persecution from flaring up. We feel safe today, but who knows what tomorrow will bring. As for tomorrow, Jesus said: "So do not worry about tomorrow; for tomorrow will care for itself. Each day has enough trouble of its own" (Matt 6:34 NASB).

Below are a few words of advice to help leaders avoid unnecessary persecution:

- Love the people you meet daily. We have found on a number of occasions that those who protect us from persecution are the very people who once did not like us. It is not your fellow believer who persuades your persecutor to stop attacking you; it is his friend who has seen your love and can speak to your persecutor, and be granted a hearing. The importance of making friends and building good relationships cannot be stressed enough for anyone who wants to serve in the Arab world.
- Visiting leaders or missionaries should always work with the local church and shadow local leaders to minimize their own persecution. The locals will understand cultural sensibilities and will be able to identify places of danger that need to be avoided.

- Proclaiming Christ boldly yet gently is always rewarding, even if the results are slow in coming. Polemical approaches that attack other faiths create animosity. Although they may seem to bear some fruit, especially among fundamentalist Muslims, they also create disruption and unnecessary social upheaval. Muslims in Lebanon, and I would argue elsewhere, are not overly concerned if an individual simply chooses to follow Christ; it is when that individual becomes a threat to the established group (a family, clan, or community) that persecution becomes more intense.

- Communicate your intention and agenda clearly. Almost every Sunday, I stand up in front of my church and remind my congregation about the purpose of what we do every week. I tell them we have no political agenda and are not a militant group; we are a church and our purpose is not to become religious but to follow Jesus more closely. We exist to make disciples. We have found a new way to live our life, a new way to become human, a new path to follow, and this path is to be conformed to the likeness of Jesus. If you want to become like Jesus, you have come to the right place.

- Differentiate between socio-cultural values and core Christian values. People in our community can still look the same, cook the same food, wear the same clothes, and retain a lot of their cultural norms and values (such as honoring their parents and submitting to one another) without compromising and losing their new identity in Christ. People do not have to look and act like Westerners to be Christians. We all know that, yet we still expect new followers of Jesus to think in a Western way, or to use Christian terms imported from the West, or to dress in a certain way. We naturally want people who share our faith to behave like us, look like us and sound like us. We should never force them to do this, but we should not stop them from becoming like us if they choose to do so. This should always be a matter of choice. It is natural that we influence one another. By reading from the same book and singing the same songs and hearing the same sermons, we start using similar terminology and become closer culturally and socially. This is unavoidable. Preachers, teachers and life group leaders should remain as close as possible to the word of God in core matters and as close as possible to their social context in peripheral matters in order to lead healthy groups and avoid unnecessary persecution.

- Demonstrate care for the whole family. Isolating one individual and sharing Christ with them is not a bad strategy, especially if you are working in a hostile environment. However, we have found that when a leader ministers to and serves the whole family, including the children, a new dynamic emerges. This person becomes the friend of the family and the children ask for him or her. Parents love it when a leader bows down and gives special consideration to their child. They find the leader humble and caring. It is good to bless children in front of their parents, to buy small gifts for them, and to show them physical affection by carrying them and kissing them on the forehead or on the cheek. It creates a new kind of bond between the family and the follower of Jesus.

- Avoid talking politics. I think this is impossible in the Arab world, but at least we can try! I personally find it hard, and I seldom manage to stay away from politics. I feel people like to know my opinion, and above all they like to tell me what they think and believe regarding politics. I have learned to speak about politics but remain positive and avoid speaking ill of a governor; to neither judge others, nor start complaining and assigning blame, as well as never to confuse facts with opinion. This positive approach can help you see politics as an entry point to building good relationships, but it can also get you into trouble.

- Expect that some people will deceive you. When you love, you choose to become vulnerable, and this may cause you pain. I once heard a pastor say that if you see a wolf coming towards you, you get ready to protect and defend yourself, but if one of your sheep comes towards you, you open your arms to receive him. If the sheep then attacks you, how much more you are hurt! When you choose to treat your enemies as friends, you may end up paying a high price.

God's Vindication

When I quoted Paul's hymn at the start of this chapter, I deliberately omitted the last verse. But now we need to hear it:

> For this reason also, God highly exalted him, and bestowed on him the name which is above every name, so that at the name of Jesus every knee will bow, of those who are in heaven and on earth and under the earth, and that every tongue will confess that Jesus Christ is Lord, to the glory of God the Father. (Phil 2:9–11)

Jesus did not stay in the grave, Jesus rose in victory. The path of following Jesus does not end at the tomb, but rather leads through the tomb towards victory. This glorious message should be a daily reality that will be fully realized upon his return.

It is wrong to think that God's vindication is solely something that will happen in the future. It has already happened on the cross and through the resurrection and ascension of Christ, and it has practical implications in our daily life. The stories of transformation and restoration in this book and in the life of every believer demonstrate the present reality and implications of God's work through Christ in us. The forgiveness of sins, peace in the midst of tribulation, boldness to witness in the midst of persecution, courage not to renounce one's faith in the face of death, acts of kindness and humility in relationships, victory over lustful and selfish ambitions, a forgiving spirit, love for all, including our enemies, miraculous healings of our bodies and souls, freedom from the evil past, self-control, the recovery of our identity, belonging to a family of God that is multi-racial and multi-ethnic, thriving in the Arab world which is predominately Muslim, and having the assurance that eternity is secured by the blood of Christ – these are all marks of vindication in our daily life.

Walking victoriously has a tremendous impact in our region, especially for those who are still rooted in the tribal way of thinking where vindication is the mark of true heroism. No one wants to follow a weak leader who died on the cross and did not rise from the dead. No one wants to follow a defeated person from another tribe. Our victorious life is the key that draws people to Christ.

Today we can live as "more than conquerors," we can live with great hope that the world will not be the same. This is not triumphalism; this is the victory of Christ in us. So we walk with confidence, but not with arrogance. We look our enemy in the eye, but we do so with compassion and love. We walk fearless of death because our eternity is secure, and because we are confident that God has the final say in all matters. We walk victoriously because we do not seek anything for ourselves, for we know that we are his children, princesses and princes of the King, the King who was born in a humble manger yet is the King of kings, who wept for Lazarus, who bent down and washed the feet of his disciples, who wore a crown of thorns, was abandoned, mocked, tortured, humiliated, shamed and was killed by the most shameful and disgraceful punishing method of crucifixion, yet remained the Son of God to whom all power and authority was given and whose name is above all other names.

A victorious life is not about what we do; it is about who we are. It is about preserving and cherishing our first love. The deeper our relationship with

Christ, the better our understanding of true victory will be. A victorious life is a humble, Christ-honoring, outward-looking, serving life. It is the freedom to choose to walk behind our Master as closely as possible, without the burden of sin, law, fear or death. It is a choice to love him unceasingly, to obey him faithfully, and to serve him at any cost.

With Paul, we say, "For the law of the Spirit of life has set you free in Christ Jesus from the law of sin and death" (Rom 8:2). How thankful we are to God who has given us "the victory through our Lord Jesus Christ" (1 Cor 15:57). So again with Paul we can say, "If then you have been raised with Christ, seek the things that are above, where Christ is, seated at the right hand of God" (Col 3:1), for he "raised us up with him and seated us with him in the heavenly places in Christ Jesus" (Eph 2:6). Finally, the day Jesus promised will come, "when the Son of Man will sit on his glorious throne [and] you who have followed me will also sit on twelve thrones, judging the twelve tribes of Israel" (Matt 19:28).

15

Pooling Our Resources

In 2011, when the war in Syria broke out and Syrians started to flee to Lebanon, we were somewhat prepared to receive them. However, the truth is that you can never really be fully prepared for any of God's movements. When God moves powerfully, we have learned to do three things: to follow his agenda and not ours; to constantly develop leaders and emerging leaders to carry out the ministry; and to partner with others. A few projects can be handled by a single church, but a movement needs churches to work together – and when we partner together, God alone receives the glory.

Sometimes we partner with local churches, and sometimes with churches in other countries, or with parachurch organizations. Such relationships can be very beneficial, or they can be damaging. So this is what we will be looking at in this chapter.

But before we talk about the options for pooling our resources with outside partners, is it very important that we look at what we can accomplish by pooling our own resources. There is a tendency in some churches in the Arab world to seek funding from outside sources first. We have also fallen prey to this. And it is a mistake.

Drawing on Our Own Resources

The New Testament makes it clear that believers should give generously in order to meet the needs of the times (Acts 2:45; 2 Cor 9:7–14); but it never says how much we should give. So at RCB we encourage believers to give weekly or monthly tithes as an act of worship and as an acknowledgement that God is the real source of all our income. We also encourage believers to give more if the Lord calls them to do so.

Giving is a voluntarily act of worship by radical disciples of Jesus. That is why we at RCB encourage everyone to give, even refugees. There is dignity in giving and sharing our resources, however little. Many refugees with virtually no income still contribute faithfully to the ministry of the church.

We have, however, made certain changes to how we give. We no longer pass an offering basket around during the service. This is partly because we wanted generosity to be part of our culture, not merely a formal part of a service. We wanted believers to make giving a priority without being told when to give. We also realized that some of our refugees, who had once been wealthy and had lost literally everything, felt embarrassed when the basket was passed around and they were unable to give. Some even yielded to the temptation to save face by pretending to put something in the basket. So we decided to place baskets at the back of the church so that those who wish to give can give whatever they chose.

Stewardship of resources is, however, about more than just giving. That is why we encourage Christian businessmen and women to educate the congregation about faithful stewardship. They can teach us about handling debt and about the accumulation and preservation of wealth, as well as about the importance of distributing wealth. They know from experience that while making money is seen as a sign of success, distributing our wealth moves us from a life of success to a life of significance. Christians with financial expertise can also help us make sure that any money given to the church is accounted for, to make sure that it is used wisely and rightly.

We also work hard to ensure that we do not develop a "donor culture." Our church is grateful for the many partners and churches that support our ministries. Without them, we could not serve the thousands of refugees and needy people who come to us. However, we do not want the people in the congregation to give less because other donors are giving too. For this reason, I tell my congregation that unless we as a church give more, we will not ask our partners to give more. Generosity has to start with us. In this way, we ensure that external funding does not hinder our own generosity. This is the only way for money to be a blessing for a church and not a curse or an excuse for not giving locally.

Working with Partners

When the need is much greater than any one church can handle alone, we seek other groups who can pool their resources with ours. RCB has a number of partnerships, one of which is Forest Hill Church in Charlotte, North Carolina, led by Pastor David Chadwick. This partnership is going very well, and both churches feel we are one family. In the course of building partnerships, we have learned that the following elements are vital to any successful partnership.

Know your calling

The humanitarian need among refugees is so great that the church is in danger of losing focus by seeking to serve everyone everywhere. Any attempt to do this imposes an intolerable burden that negatively impacts everyone involved. So at RCB we have carefully defined our task. Rather than being involved in food distribution on a massive scale, we have chosen to invest holistically in families in need. The church is not just a food bank for the body; the church is a "hospital" for an entire human being.

Once the church leadership had embraced this holistic mission, we worked to create a culture of generosity by taking the lead in giving abundantly to the mission of the church and to the service of the community. Only then, once we had a clear view of our mission and our capacities, was it the right time to initiate partnerships.

Know your partner

The church should be careful whom it works with. As mentioned earlier, there are some donor organizations that are only interested in head counts. The unspoken (or spoken) question is, "If I give you this money, how many souls will be saved?" This question reflects both bad theology and a lack of commitment to holistic mission.

So when talks about partnership begin, the focus should not be solely on funding. Before that point even comes up, the participants should all be able to answer the "why" question: Why are we talking about doing this? The "what" and "how" questions should come later. Moreover, everyone involved should believe that all are partnering with God equally, sharing in the privilege of working together to spread God's kingdom in different parts of the world. No partner should feel intimidated because another partner has more financial resources. Nor should a lack of funds lead to leaders being aggressive and making demands. We should share with passion and boldness about our ministries, but in a way that gives our partners the freedom to say no without feeling embarrassed about letting us down.

Meanwhile the donors and organizational leaders should genuinely listen to the need of the church by asking and observing. They should not come with a list of what they plan to do, but to ask whether the church needs any help and whether their organization can help and in what capacity.

Prior to making any financial commitment, donors should build strong relationships. When money follows good relationships, it bears good results in the long-term; when money precedes good relationships, it can cause problems or at best bear short-term results. What is needed is an invitation to friendship in a long-term partnership in kingdom business that offers a threefold blessing: a blessing on the Western church, a blessing on the local church, and a blessing on the communities we serve.

Agree on methods

It is vital that the organization that we partner with be committed to working with the church. Unfortunately, many parachurch organizations fail to do this. Instead of supporting the local church, they set out to work independently and do great harm to the church. While I cannot think of a single Christian organization that intentionally sets out to hurt the local church, here are some all-too-common examples of how the way they operate can do exactly that:

- Hiring key leaders to work for their organizations, and so emptying the church of its human resources.
- Going around criticizing the church for losing its vision and not being able to serve its community.
- Expecting church leaders to always be available for visits to those who donate food packages. After all, why should a pastor be so occupied with shepherding and feeding his sheep that he does not have the luxury to travel around and spend more than half his time fundraising?
- Imposing programs and curricula on the local church that serve the parachurch organization's own needs.
- Bypassing the leadership of the church and constantly inviting emerging leaders to attend training and conferences, thus affecting their ministry in their local churches.
- Disrupting the make-up of a church leadership team by providing financial support to only some leaders, and offering them the option of transferring their loyalty to a group with more funding. We have seen many leaders and church teams become rebellious and unaccountable in these circumstances.
- Inviting inexperienced missionaries to come and work for Western organizations with no local accountability. Their naivety has put the ministry of the churches they attend in jeopardy.

When their projects finish, organizations that work in this way leave behind a dying church.

A far better way to go about things is for the partner organization or churches to take the lead in identifying effective local churches. They can then ask the leaders of these local churches whether they can serve and stand by them with no pre-prepared agenda. If their offer is accepted, they can work with the local church to draw up a strategic plan, preferably long-term, that serves the need of the local church and the community. Where possible, this plan should not involve parachuting in missionaries. Instead, careful consideration should be given to sponsoring local leaders to carry out the mission.

We have noticed an interesting phenomenon when we have presented requests for sponsorship in the past. Quite often, the reply we get goes along the lines of "we don't want the church to become dependent. It would be better to send some of our people to work for you as missionaries for a while." But why does supporting missionaries not create dependency whereas financial funding does? Is it because missionaries are ineffective and so don't create dependency for local churches? Some missionaries in my church are highly effective and to see them go is a real loss. Others could be effective but choose to simply attend church and do the minimum "so as not to create dependency on the West." Still others are ineffective and would do their churches a favour by returning home.

Sending missionaries is only helpful when they are requested by the local church and not when they simply show up: "Hello Pastor, my name in John, this is my wife and my two girls. My family and I are called to be with you to train your leaders to become more effective in their ministry. . . . meanwhile we will be studying Arabic and will learn more about your wonderful culture." Great motive but wrong execution. We do need missionaries – some to pray, others to shadow and mentor, and others to equip, train and serve – but please let the need drive the hiring process. We don't want to waste people's time and resources for no fruitful purpose. We cannot afford to have the wrong missionaries with the wrong skills doing what they thought was the right thing to do. Sadly they become a burden, they get frustrated, they feel unwelcomed, and they get depressed. We have seen families collapse as a result of a wrong decision. Let's do it together. Let the need drive the process.

Why not sponsor local leaders? They have the linguistic and practical skills to serve their own people but lack financial resources because of the context in which they live. The Western church has financial and professional resources but lacks linguistic and practical resources. Why not join together in more effective and fruitful service? Equipping key potential leaders who are recommended by the leadership team of the local church is a wonderful way of creating long-term sustainability and effectiveness.

What Can We Do?

Some of you who are reading this book will now be asking, what can I do? How can I help with ministry in the Arab world? Do I have a role? Does my church have a role?

Yes of course you do. All that has been said so far is intended to give you wisdom as you go about doing this. Here are some suggestions:

- Western pastors and church leaders who have the means but are unable to serve in the Arab world, should consider partnering with local churches on a deeper level. They should prayerfully seek churches that have a clear vision but lack human, professional or financial resources to accomplish that vision.
- Church members who choose to give only to NGOs should reconsider their giving strategy and start giving to local churches who partner closely with other local churches on the ground.
- Once relationships and trust are established, Christians can serve congregations in the Arab world from their homes and from a distance. Audio-visual experts, social media professionals, website designers, program developers, IT and financial specialists, cross-cultural coaches and counsellors, and church leaders can do a lot through online communication to help, train and serve from a distance. This does not work in all situations, especially if there is a language barrier, but it can sometimes be very effective and can cut expenses significantly.
- Sending short- or long-term missionaries to shadow leaders and encourage them is a wonderful way of serving together while still letting local leaders take the lead in serving their own people. Ministries could include education, counselling and prayer, discipleship, food programs, winterization, medical services, social clubs and training in various skills.

Finally, remember that ministry is not a one-way street. Churches like RCB, and others experienced in ministering to refugees, can be of great service in providing training, methodology and an understanding of cultural and language barriers to churches in the West that are embarking on refugee ministry.

Epilogue

Throughout this book we have returned time and time again to the hymn to Christ's ultimate love and faithful obedience in Philippians 2. That hymn was on the opening page of this book, and it is on our minds as we end it. There Paul presents Christ as our model. The life of love is perfectly shown in Christ's ultimate love as demonstrated on the cross. That is why forgiving and sacrificially loving one another should characterize the followers of Jesus in their relationships with one another.

During the long years of the Lebanese civil war, I and others lost many friends and relatives. Our country was at the mercy of a ruthless Syrian regime. Many who are alive today remember the Syrians who raped our women, killed our children and destroyed our homes. The sights we saw are still vivid in our minds: the intense fires, the screaming children, the smell of smoke as the bombs exploded.

When the Syrian war began and the Syrian refugees began to arrive, the thoughts of many turned to revenge. Thankfully not all held this view. How can those who have deeply experienced the grace, peace and love of Christ, seek revenge? If you have put on Christ, the full embodiment of sacrificial love, then you are what you love. The love in you cannot hate. Many Muslims have come to us and asked why we love them, how we can serve them, what is driving us to do all of this? It is Christ-like character that is drawing Muslims to Jesus. I cannot think of a stronger weapon than love. It is much more powerful than the most sophisticated weaponry.

Earlier in this book, I mentioned the mothers who came to me and said, "I don't want my children to play with their children"; "I don't want my children to go to the same toilets as theirs"; "The person who sat next to me smells differently and talks differently"; "Our church has become unbearable." How do we respond to these concerns?

Before we answer this question, we should ask what kind of disciples we are raising up in our churches if the women have such feelings? Is Christian education merely about head knowledge, or is it about love? Why have all our sermons only impacted the head and not the heart and hands? Maybe we should reconsider our discipleship methods. Maybe they have not seen a better model, or there is no one to imitate.

I was pondering these questions, when God challenged me and said that if the congregation is not loving, then maybe it is because we as leaders are not loving either. I had to do something about it. I had to change. I needed to start loving in a practical way if I wanted the congregation to see that I loved these people deeply.

So one day, I took my own children down to an area where many refugees live and we visited a few families and took their kids to buy them toys. It was transformational for all of us, and I shared my experience with the church. On other occasions, I took leaders with me to visit refugee homes – none returned the same. I truly believe that a congregation mirrors its leaders. If they are not kind to strangers, it is because they are imitating us, their leaders. A Christ-like character is essential, and from the overflow deeds follow.

One of our most moving Sunday services took place a few years ago when, during the service, I invited a key Syrian leader in the community who had come to faith to come forward in front of the congregation. Then I began to wash his feet. By this act I as a representative of my church was showing that we choose to express genuine love and have an unwavering willingness to serve the Syrian refugee community, whom we consider our brothers and sisters. He in return, as a leader representing his community, showed how to receive with humility our love and desire to serve.

It was a moving experience for all. I was not expecting it to touch me as deeply as it did – I thought I was prepared for it and it was going to be like all other sermon illustrations, but this one was different. When I bowed down and lifted his foot up and started to wash and clean it with love, heaven opened and the Spirit came and dwelt among us. The congregation did not know whether to clap or wipe away their tears. God was pleased with his church, and I felt an indescribable joy and a deep contentment.

That event is well remembered and many describe it as the moment that a very old wall came crashing down and a new bridge was built between our two communities.

May you and I continue to break down walls, build bridges, and grow disciples of our one and only Lord!

Appendix:
The Pathway of Following Jesus

New believers in our church are encouraged to take a six session course that constitutes a pathway to discipleship. It covers some basic principles of the Christian life that apply in all cultures, but is presented in a way that speaks to believers from Arab cultures. This book provides some guidelines on how that can be done.

Before you look at the details of this course, I would again like to stress that this pathway is not to be presented merely as part of a program but is part of a lifestyle. The course will often be studied by small groups of new believers led by an experienced small group leader who will walk alongside them while they take this course and remain with them after it is complete.

Session 1: Believing – an introduction to what it means to believe in Jesus, focusing on (1) freely choosing to trust in him (faith), (2) turning away from our previous way of life (repentance), and (3) choosing to follow him.

Session 2: Being Filled – an introduction to the Holy Spirit who comes (1) to dwell in us, (2) develop his fruit in us, and (3) pour out his gifts on us.

Session 3: Crowning – an introduction to what it means to crown Jesus Lord over our life: (1) over our time (daily devotion as a sign of the lordship of Christ over our time), (2) over our relationships (belonging to a life-group as a sign of crowning Jesus lord over our relationships), and (3) over our resources (tithes and offerings as a sign of faithful stewardship).

Session 4: Belonging – an introduction to the importance of belonging to Christ's church, in which we discuss things like (1) shared faith (the Nicene Creed, baptism, the Lord's Supper), (2) shared culture (our mission and vision, symbols, and values), and (3) shared structure.

Session 5: Witnessing about Christ – We do this (1) through holy words (some guidelines on how to talk about our faith, covering respectful dialogue, proclamation of Christ, and basic apologetics, stressing that we need to be able to answer gently and respectfully when questioned about our beliefs), (2) through holy deeds (we follow Jesus's example of "inviting," "teaching," "setting free," "healing," and "praying"), (3) through a holy life (a study based on Philippians 2:5–11 in which we stress the call to be like Christ and manifest the virtues of humility and unconditional love [a self-giving life], knowing that they are the keys to a victorious life).

Session 6: Making Disciples – a reminder that we are not just called to be disciples but also (1) to call others to imitate us as we imitate Christ, (2) to equip them through teaching and instruction, through fellowship and partnership, and through spiritual disciplines and experiences, and (3) to send them to the world to do the same.

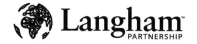 **Langham**
PARTNERSHIP

Langham Literature, with its publishing work, is a ministry of Langham Partnership.

Langham Partnership is a global fellowship working in pursuit of the vision God entrusted to its founder John Stott –

> *to facilitate the growth of the church in maturity and Christ-likeness through raising the standards of biblical preaching and teaching.*

Our vision is to see churches in the majority world equipped for mission and growing to maturity in Christ through the ministry of pastors and leaders who believe, teach and live by the Word of God.

Our mission is to strengthen the ministry of the Word of God through:
- nurturing national movements for biblical preaching
- fostering the creation and distribution of evangelical literature
- enhancing evangelical theological education

especially in countries where churches are under-resourced.

Our ministry

Langham Preaching partners with national leaders to nurture indigenous biblical preaching movements for pastors and lay preachers all around the world. With the support of a team of trainers from many countries, a multi-level programme of seminars provides practical training, and is followed by a programme for training local facilitators. Local preachers' groups and national and regional networks ensure continuity and ongoing development, seeking to build vigorous movements committed to Bible exposition.

Langham Literature provides majority world preachers, scholars and seminary libraries with evangelical books and electronic resources through publishing and distribution, grants and discounts. The programme also fosters the creation of indigenous evangelical books in many languages, through writer's grants, strengthening local evangelical publishing houses, and investment in major regional literature projects, such as one volume Bible commentaries like the *Africa Bible Commentary* and the *South Asia Bible Commentary*.

Langham Scholars provides financial support for evangelical doctoral students from the majority world so that, when they return home, they may train pastors and other Christian leaders with sound, biblical and theological teaching. This programme equips those who equip others. Langham Scholars also works in partnership with majority world seminaries in strengthening evangelical theological education. A growing number of Langham Scholars study in high quality doctoral programmes in the majority world itself. As well as teaching the next generation of pastors, graduated Langham Scholars exercise significant influence through their writing and leadership.

To learn more about Langham Partnership and the work we do visit **langham.org**

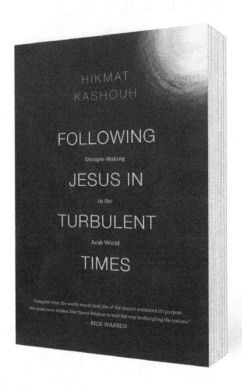

FOLLOWING JESUS IN TURBULENT TIMES: DISCIPLE-MAKING IN THE ARAB WORLD

HIKMAT KASHOUH

9781783685134 | October 2018 | Paperback | 152 pages

SPECIAL MINISTRY DISCOUNTS:

50–100 copies - 20% discount
100–300 copies - 30% discount
300+ copies - 40% discount

Free International Shipping
on all orders

Email orders to literature@langham.org or call +44 1228 592 033 quoting the ministry discount

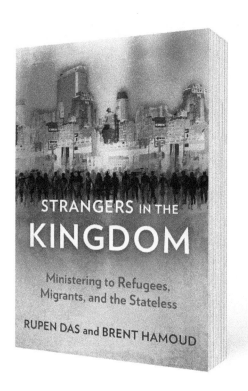

STRANGERS IN THE KINGDOM:
MINISTERING TO REFUGEES, MIGRANTS, AND THE STATELESS

RUPEN DAS and BRENT HAMOUD

9781783682775 | May 2017 | Paperback | 144 pages

SPECIAL MINISTRY DISCOUNTS:

50–100 copies - 20% discount
100–300 copies - 30% discount
300+ copies - 40% discount

Free International Shipping
on all orders

Email orders to literature@langham.org or call +44 1228 592 033 quoting the ministry discount